PHILIP'S *Red Books*

LOCAL STREET ATLAS

WEYMOU
DORCHESTE

BROADMAYNE · CHARMINSTER · CHICKERELL
CROSSWAYS · FORTUNESWELL · PRESTON
PUDDLETOWN · SOUTHWELL

CONTENTS

LEGEND

	orway
	v Route
	' Road
	Minor Road
	Pedestrianized / Restricted Access
	Track
	Built Up Area
	Footpath
	Stream
	River
Lock	Canal
	Railway / Station
●	Post Office
P P+	Car Park / Park & Ride
C	Public Convenience
+	Place of Worship
→	One-way Street
i	Tourist Information Centre
▲8 ▲8	Adjoining Pages
	Area Depicting Enlarged Centre
	Emergency Services
	Industrial Buildings
	Leisure Buildings
	Education Buildings
	Hotels etc.
	Retail Buildings
	General Buildings
	Woodland
	Orchard
	Recreational / Parkland
	Cemetery

www.philips-maps.co.uk

First published in 2000 by
Estate Publications

This edition published by Philip's,
a division of Octopus Publishing Group Ltd
www.octopusbooks.co.uk
2–4 Heron Quays, London E14 4JP
An Hachette Livre UK Company

First Philip's Edition 2008
First impression 2008
08/04-08

ISBN 978-0-540-09391-5

© Philip's 2008

This product includes mapping data licensed
from Ordnance Survey®, with the permission
of the Controller of Her Majesty's Stationery
Office.© Crown copyright 2008. All rights
reserved. Licence number 100011710

Scale: 2½ Miles to 1 Inc

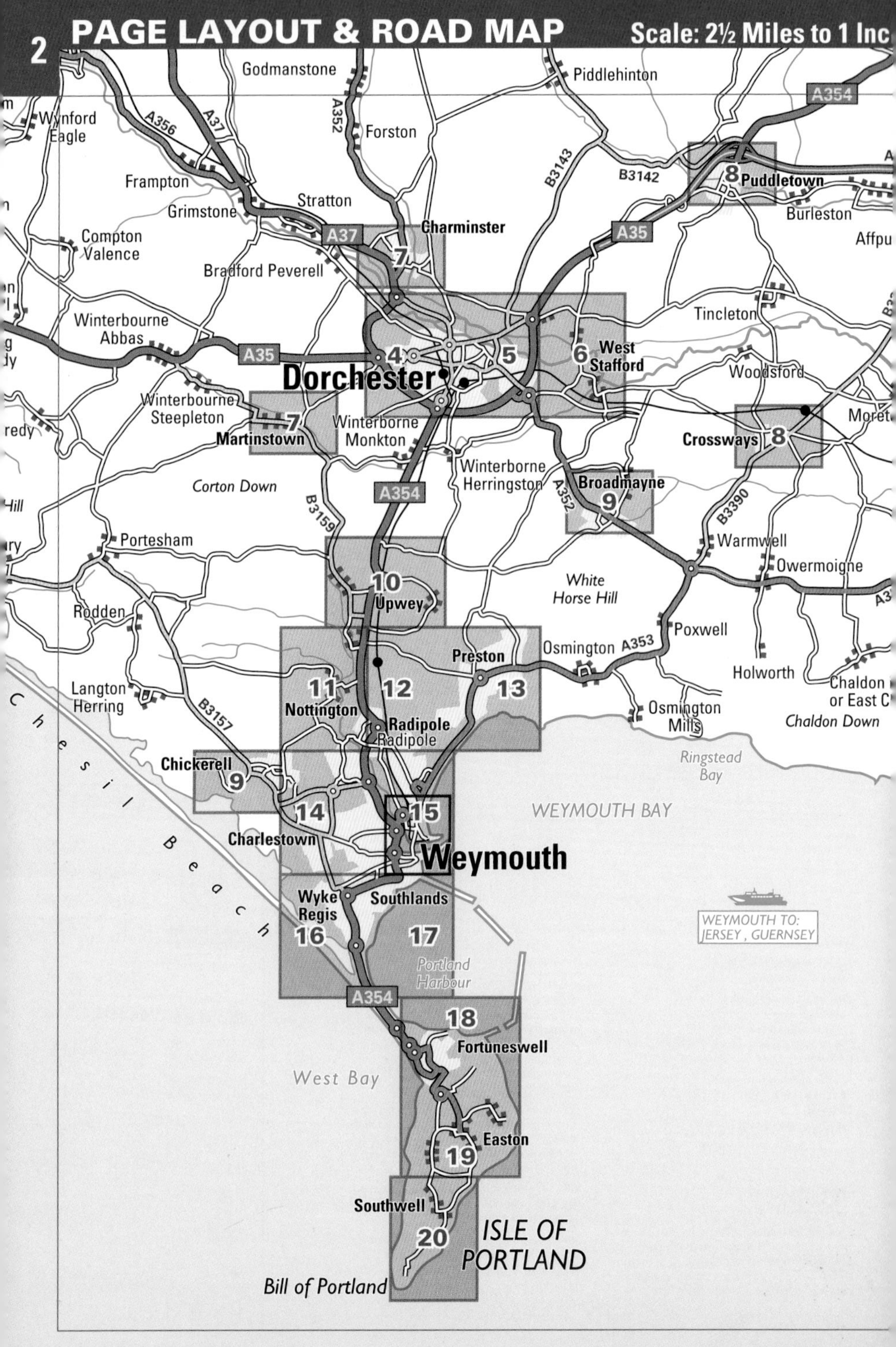
Godmanstone
Piddlehinton
A354
Wynford Eagle
A356
A37
A352
Forston
B3143
B3142
8 Puddletown
Frampton
Stratton
Grimstone
Burleston
Charminster
A35
Compton Valence
A37
7
Affpu
Bradford Peverell
Tincleton
Winterbourne Abbas
A35
4
5
6 West Stafford
Woodsford
Dorchester
Winterbourne Steepleton
7 Martinstown
Winterborne Monkton
Crossways 8
Moret
Winterborne Herringston
A352
Broadmayne 9
Corton Down
A354
B3159
B3390
Portesham
Warmwell
Owermoigne
10 Upwey
White Horse Hill
Rodden
Poxwell
Osmington A353
Preston
Holworth
Langton Herring
11
12
13
Chaldon or East C
Nottington
Radipole
Osmington Mills
Chaldon Down
B3157
Chesil Beach
Ringstead Bay
Chickerell 9
14
15
WEYMOUTH BAY
Charlestown
Weymouth
Wyke Regis
Southlands
16
17
WEYMOUTH TO: JERSEY , GUERNSEY
Portland Harbour
A354
18
Fortuneswell
West Bay
Easton
19
Southwell
20
ISLE OF PORTLAND
Bill of Portland

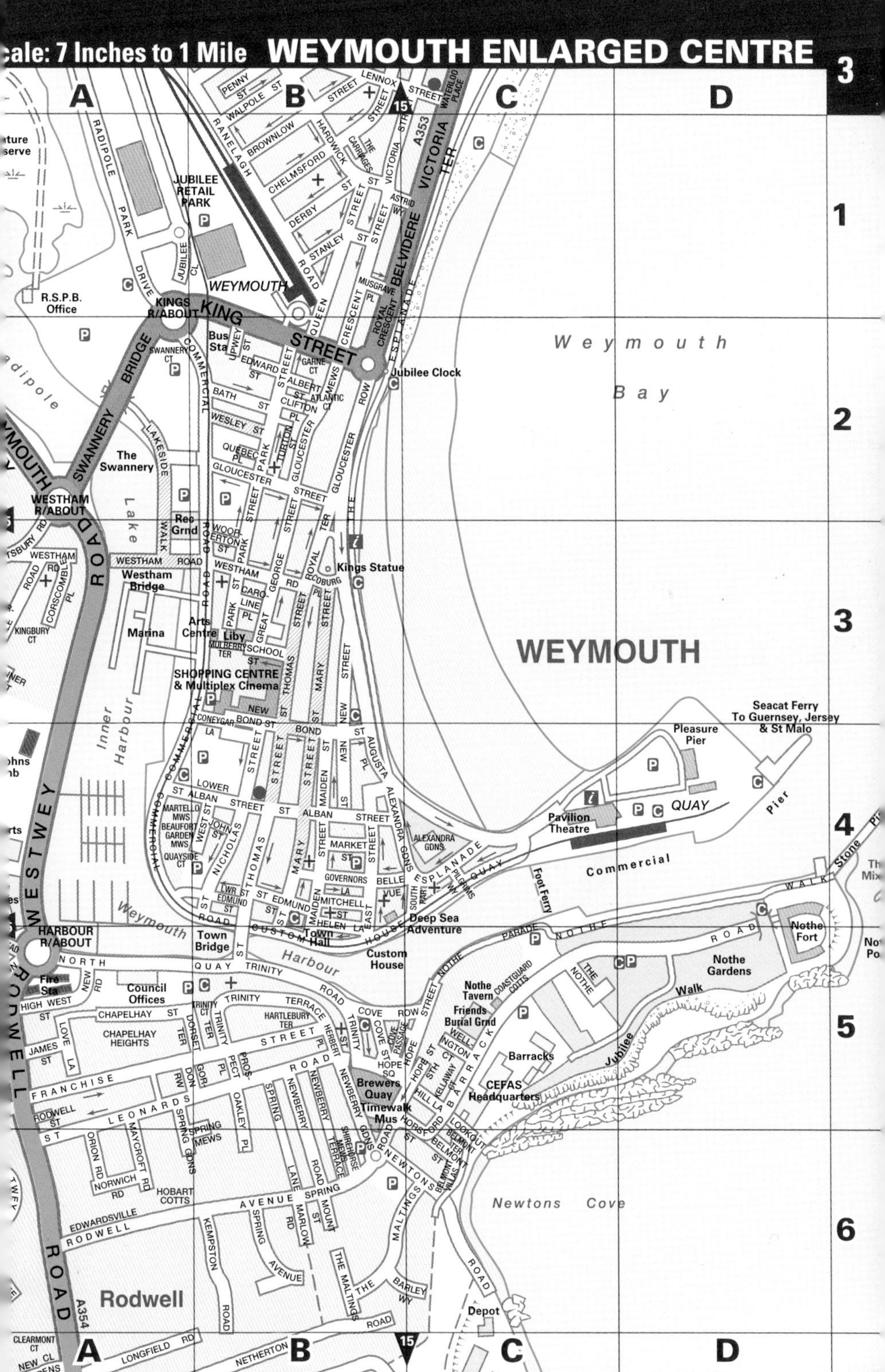
A
B
C
D
1
2
3
4
5
6
WEYMOUTH
Weymouth Bay
JUBILEE RETAIL PARK
WEYMOUTH
R.S.P.B. Office
KINGS R/ABOUT
KING STREET
Bus Sta
Jubilee Clock
The Swannery
WESTHAM R/ABOUT
SWANNERY BRIDGE
Radipole Lake
Rec Grnd
Westham Bridge
Marina
Arts Centre
Liby
Kings Statue
SHOPPING CENTRE & Multiplex Cinema
Inner Harbour
WESTWEY ROAD
Seacat Ferry To Guernsey, Jersey & St Malo
Pleasure Pier
Pavilion Theatre
QUAY
Commercial
Stone Pier
Foot Ferry
Deep Sea Adventure
Custom House
Town Hall
Town Bridge
Weymouth Harbour
HARBOUR R/ABOUT
Fire Sta
Council Offices
NOTHE PARADE
Nothe Fort
Nothe Gardens
Jubilee Walk
Nothe Tavern
Friends Burial Grnd
Barracks
CEFAS Headquarters
Brewers Quay Timewalk Mus
CHAPELHAY HEIGHTS
Newtons Cove
Depot
Rodwell
RODWELL ROAD
A354
A353
VICTORIA TER
BELVIDERE
ESPLANADE
ROYAL CRESCENT
GLOUCESTER ROW
THE ESPLANADE
ST THOMAS STREET
ST MARY STREET
NEW BOND ST
LOWER ST ALBAN STREET
COMMERCIAL ROAD
NORTH QUAY
TRINITY ROAD
HIGH WEST ST
FRANCHISE ST
ST LEONARDS RD
RODWELL AVENUE
EDWARDSVILLE
LONGFIELD RD
NETHERTON ROAD
15

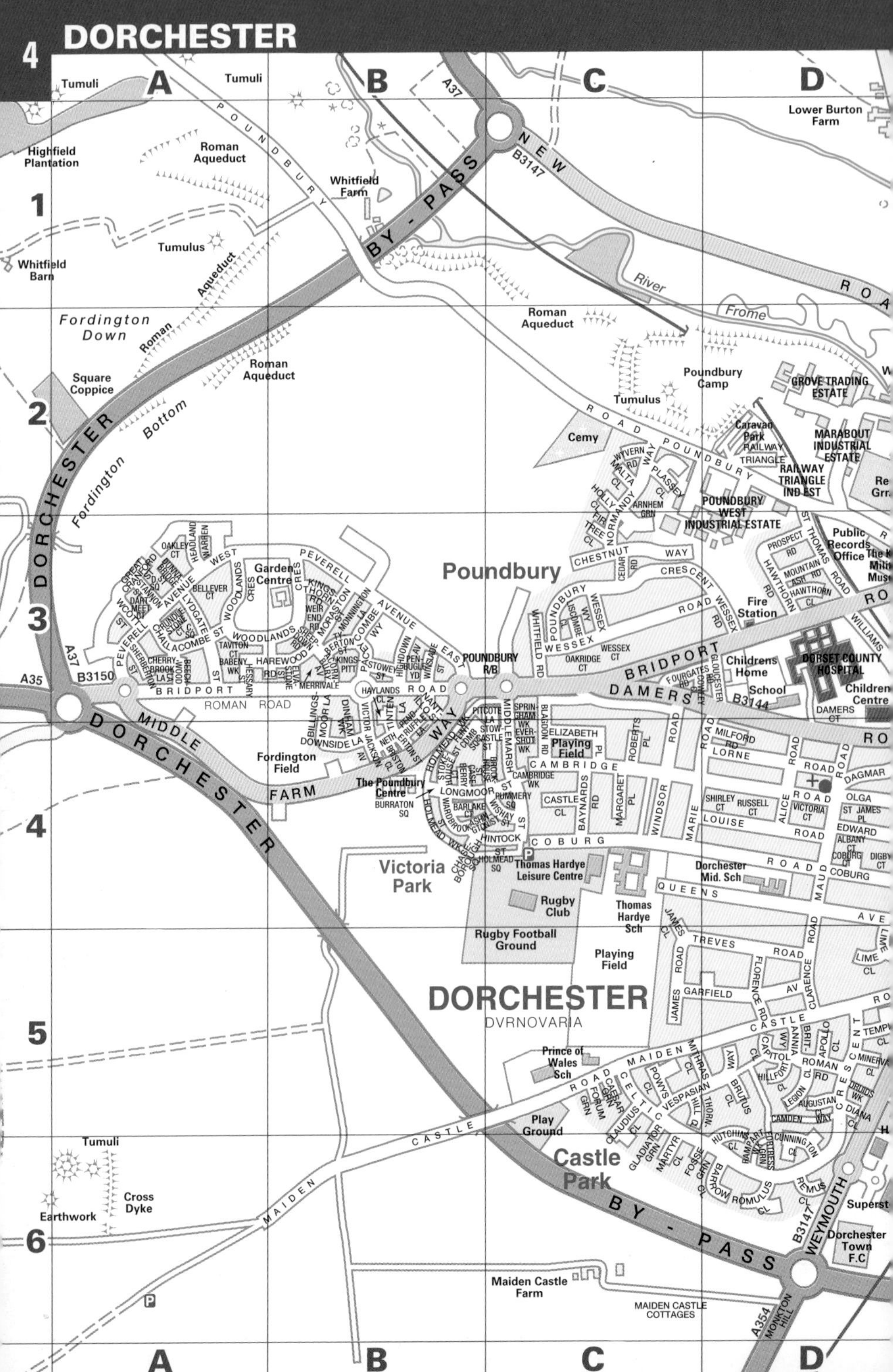
A
B
C
D
1
2
3
4
5
6
Tumuli
Highfield Plantation
Roman Aqueduct
Whitfield Farm
Whitfield Barn
Tumulus
Lower Burton Farm
Fordington Down
Square Coppice
Fordington Bottom
Poundbury Camp
Cemy
GROVE TRADING ESTATE
MARABOUT INDUSTRIAL ESTATE
RAILWAY TRIANGLE IND EST
POUNDBURY WEST INDUSTRIAL ESTATE
Public Records Office
Poundbury
Garden Centre
Fire Station
Childrens Home
School
DORSET COUNTY HOSPITAL
POUNDBURY R/B
Fordington Field
The Poundbury Centre
Playing Field
Victoria Park
Thomas Hardye Leisure Centre
Rugby Club
Rugby Football Ground
Thomas Hardye Sch
Dorchester Mid. Sch
DORCHESTER
DVRNOVARIA
Prince of Wales Sch
Play Ground
Castle Park
Earthwork
Cross Dyke
Maiden Castle Farm
MAIDEN CASTLE COTTAGES
Dorchester Town F.C
BY-PASS
DORCHESTER
MIDDLE FARM WAY
BRIDPORT ROAD
ROMAN ROAD
DAMERS RD
POUNDBURY ROAD
MAIDEN CASTLE ROAD
WEYMOUTH AVE
A37
A35
B3150
B3147
B3144
A354

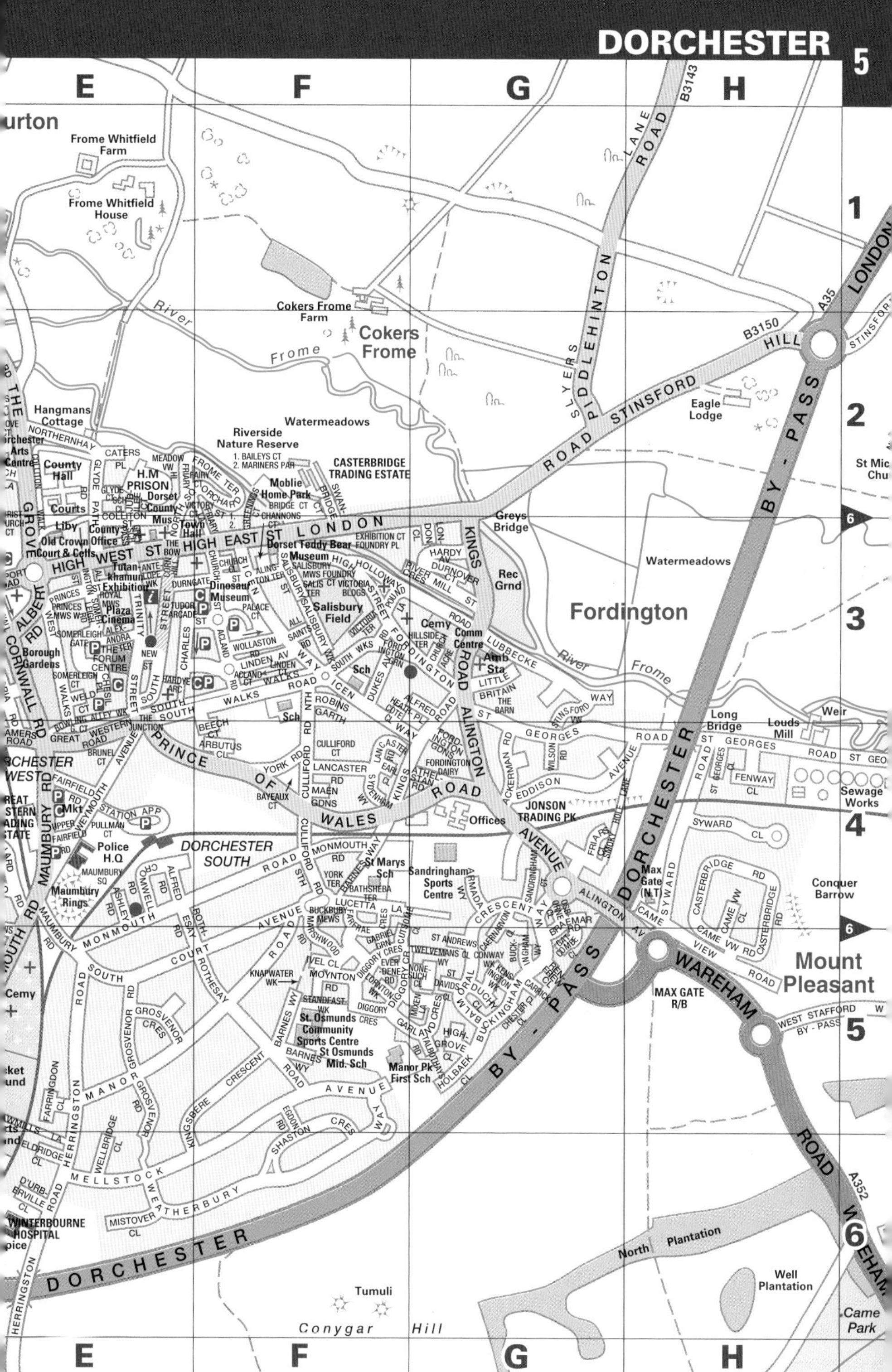

E
F
G
H
1
2
3
4
5
6
Frome Whitfield Farm
Frome Whitfield House
Cokers Frome Farm
Cokers Frome
River Frome
Hangmans Cottage
Watermeadows
Riverside Nature Reserve
CASTERBRIDGE TRADING ESTATE
Moblie Home Park
H.M PRISON
County Hall
Courts
Dorset County Mus
Town Hall
Dorset Teddy Bear Museum
Tutankhamun Exhibition
Dinosaur Museum
Plaza Cinema
Salisbury Field
Borough Gardens
Greys Bridge
Rec Grnd
Fordington
Cemy
Comm Centre
Amb Sta
Eagle Lodge
Long Bridge
Louds Mill
Weir
Sewage Works
JONSON TRADING PK
Offices
DORCHESTER SOUTH
DORCHESTER WEST
Police H.Q
Maumbury Rings
St Marys Sch
Sandringham Sports Centre
Max Gate (N.T)
MAX GATE R/B
Conquer Barrow
Mount Pleasant
St. Osmunds Community Sports Centre
St Osmunds Mid. Sch
Manor Pk First Sch
WINTERBOURNE HOSPITAL
North Plantation
Well Plantation
Came Park
Tumuli
Conygar Hill
DORCHESTER BY-PASS
LONDON ROAD
WAREHAM ROAD
STINSFORD HILL
PRINCE OF WALES ROAD
HIGH EAST ST
HIGH WEST ST
B3143
B3150
A35
A352

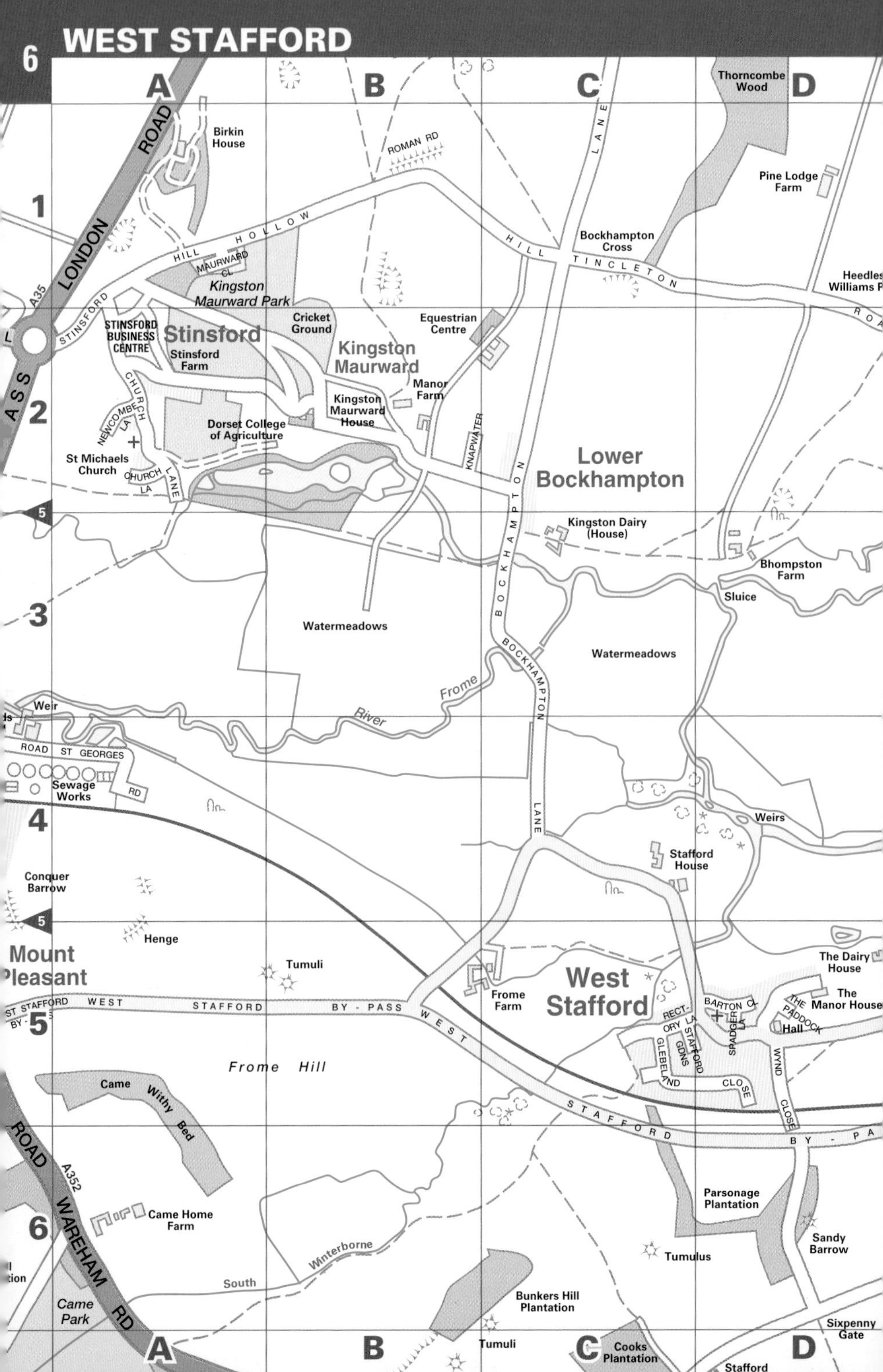

A   B   C   D

Thorncombe Wood

LONDON ROAD

Birkin House

ROMAN RD

Pine Lodge Farm

1

HILL HOLLOW

Bockhampton Cross

Heedless Williams F

MAURWARD CL

Kingston Maurward Park

HILL

TINCLETON

ROAD

STINSFORD

STINSFORD BUSINESS CENTRE

Stinsford

Stinsford Farm

Cricket Ground

Equestrian Centre

Kingston Maurward

NEWCOMBE LA

CHURCH LANE

2

St Michaels Church

CHURCH LA

Dorset College of Agriculture

Kingston Maurward House

Manor Farm

KNAPWATER

Lower Bockhampton

Kingston Dairy (House)

Bhompston Farm

Sluice

3

Watermeadows

BOCKHAMPTON

BOCKHAMPTON

Watermeadows

River Frome

LANE

Weir

ROAD ST GEORGES

Sewage Works

RD

Weirs

4

Stafford House

Conquer Barrow

Henge

Tumuli

The Dairy House

Mount Pleasant

ST STAFFORD BY

WEST STAFFORD BY-PASS

WEST

Frome Farm

West Stafford

The Manor House

RECTORY LA

STAFFORD GDNS

BARTON CL

SPADGERS LA

THE PADDOCK

Hall

5

Frome Hill

STAFFORD

GLEBELAND

CLOSE

WYND

CLOSE

BY-PA

Came

Withy Bed

Parsonage Plantation

ROAD

A352 WAREHAM RD

Came Home Farm

Winterborne

Tumulus

Sandy Barrow

6

Came Park

South

Bunkers Hill Plantation

Sixpenny Gate

Tumuli

Cooks Plantation

Stafford

A   B   C   D

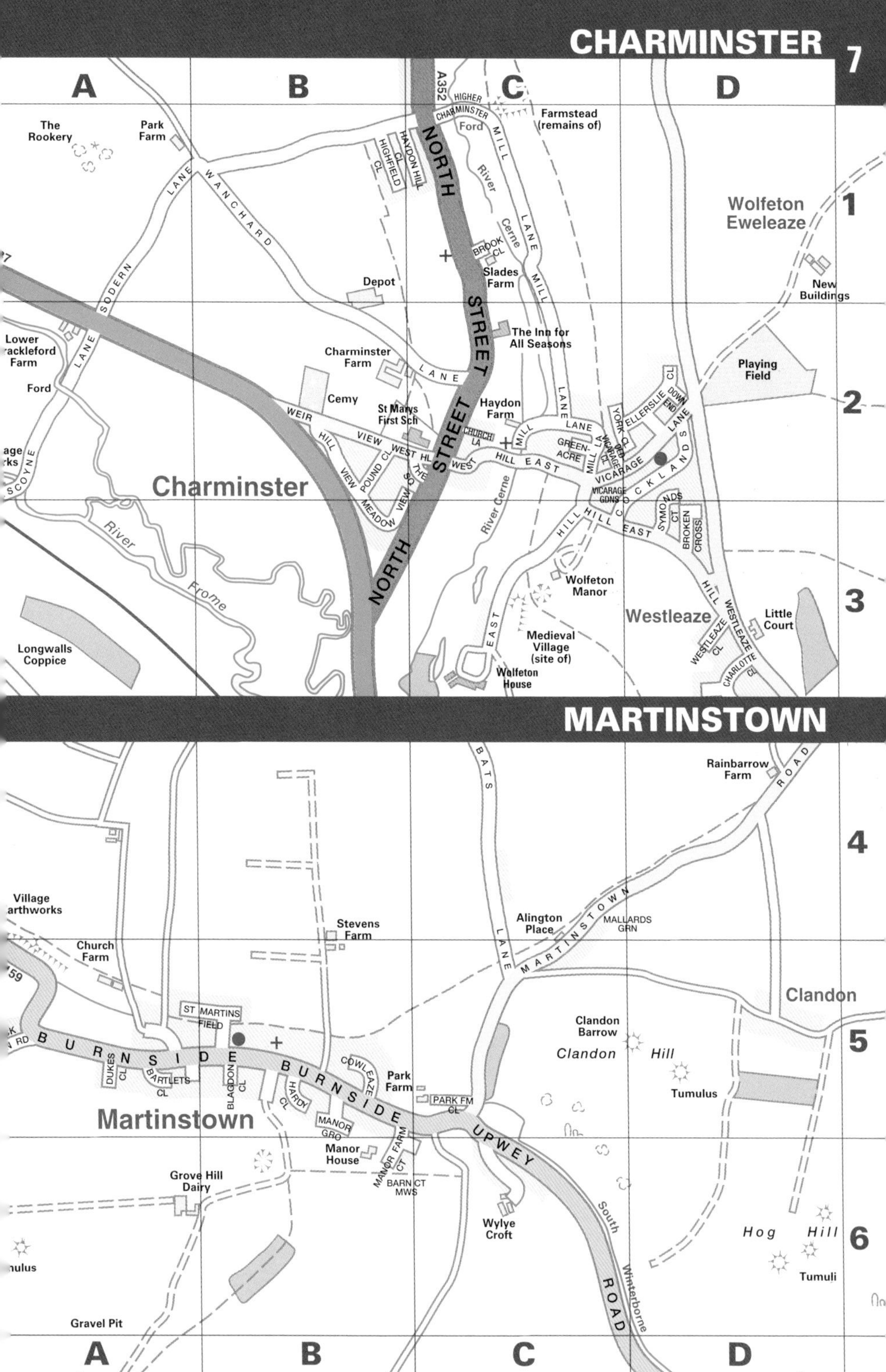

MARTINSTOWN

Charminster (top map)

A352

The Rookery

Park Farm

WANCHARD LANE

LANE SODERN

HAYDON HILL

HIGHFIELD CL

Depot

HIGHER CHARMINSTER Ford

Farmstead (remains of)

Wolfeton Eweleaze

New Buildings

NORTH STREET

River Cerne

MILL River

Slades Farm

BROOK CL

CERNE MILL LANE

The Inn for All Seasons

Playing Field

Lower Frackleford Farm

Ford

Charminster Farm

Cemy

St Marys First Sch

Haydon Farm

GREEN-ACRE

VICARAGE GDNS

YORK TERR

LICHETT

MILL LANE

ELLERSLIE CL

DOWN END

BACKLANDS

SYMONDS CT

BROKEN CROSS

WEIR

CHURCH LA

POUND CL

WEST HL

WEST VIEW

VIEW CL

WEST VIEW MEADOW

HILL VIEW

Charminster

River Frome

NORTH STREET

River Cerne

HILL EAST

Longwalls Coppice

EAST

Medieval Village (site of)

Wolfeton Manor

Wolfeton House

Westleaze

WESTLEAZE CL

CHARLOTTE CL

Little Court

Martinstown (bottom map)

Village earthworks

Church Farm

A59

BATS

Rainbarrow Farm

ROAD

Stevens Farm

Alington Place

MARTINSTOWN LANE

MALLARDS GRN

Clandon

ST MARTINS FIELD

BURNSIDE

DUKES CL

BARTLETTS CL

BLAGDON CL

HARDY CL

COWLEAZE

Park Farm

PARK FM CL

UPWEY

Clandon Barrow

Clandon Hill

Tumulus

Martinstown

MANOR GRO

MANOR FARM

BARN CT MWS

Manor House

Grove Hill Dairy

Wylye Croft

South Winterborne

ROAD

Hog Hill

Tumuli

Tumulus

Gravel Pit

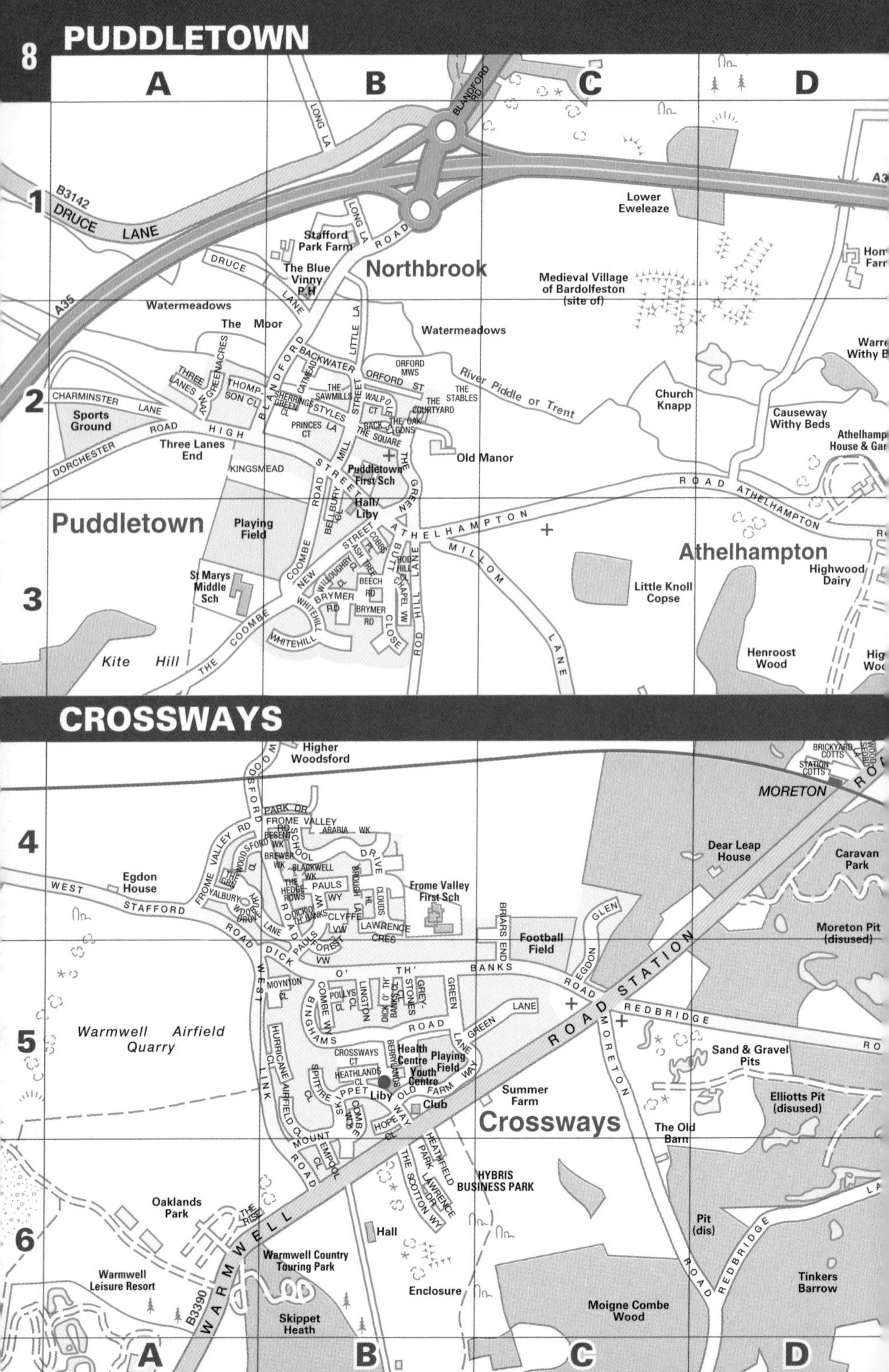

A   **B**   **C**   **D**

1

B3142
DRUCE LANE
DRUCE LANE
A35
BLANDFORD RD
LONG LA
LONG RD

Stafford Park Farm
The Blue Vinny P.H
Watermeadows
Northbrook

Lower Eweleaze

A3

Medieval Village of Bardolfeston (site of)

Hom Farr

Warre Withy B

2

CHARMINSTER LANE
Sports Ground
THREE LANES
GREENACRES
THOMP SON CL
HIGH
DORCHESTER ROAD
Three Lanes End
KINGSMEAD
The Moor
The Moor
BLANDFORD RD
BACKWATER
OATWAY
BANKS
BLANDINGS GREEN
THE SAWMILLS
THE STYLES
PRINCES LA
CT
THE SQUARE
MILL STREET
LITTLE LA
ORFORD ST
ORFORD MWS
WALPO
BACK LA
THE GDNS
THE COURTYARD
The Oak
Old Manor
The Stables
Watermeadows
River Piddle or Trent
Church Knapp
Causeway Withy Beds
Athelhamp House & Gar

Puddletown
Playing Field
Puddletown First Sch
Hall/ Liby
St Marys Middle Sch
BELLBURY CT
STRETTON
COOMBE
NEW STREET
WILLOUGHBY
BRAYMER RD
WHITEHILL
BEECH RD
BRYMER RD
CLOSE
THE GREEN
ATHELHAMPTON
CHAPEL WAY
ASH HILL
WOOD HILL
CAPEL LA
ROAD ATHELHAMPTON
MILLOM LANE

Athelhampton

Highwood Dairy
Little Knoll Copse
Henroost Wood
Highwood Wood

3

Kite Hill
THE COOMBE
WHITEHILL

R

Higher Woodsford
WOODSFORD RD

BRICKYARD COTTS
STATION COTTS
WODS ROA
MORETON
RO

4

WEST STAFFORD
Egdon House
FROME VALLEY RD
PARK DR
FROME VALLEY
ARABIA WK
BESSANT WK
BREWER WK
THE CLOSE
YALBURY LANE
FROME VALLEY RD
WOODSFORD RD
FROME VALLEY DRIVE
BLACKWELL WK
THE HEDGE ROWS
PAULS WY
CHURCH BANKS
DICK O'PAULS LANE
CLYFFE WY
LAWRENCE CRES
CLOUDS WY
FOREST WY
Frome Valley First Sch

BRIARS END
Football Field
GLEN
Dear Leap House
Caravan Park
Moreton Pit (disused)

MORETON STATION ROAD

5

Warmwell Airfield Quarry

MOYNTON CL
HURRICANE CL
SPITFIRE CL
WARMWELL AIRFIELD LINK
MOUNT ROAD
BINGHAMS
BINGHAM
COOMBE WAY
TH' STONES
LINGTON HL
POLLYS CL
GREY- CL
PICKET CL
CROSSWAYS CT
HEATHLANDS
HEATHLANDS CL
EMPOOL CL
HOPE CL
BERRY WY
WAY
Health Centre
Youth Centre
Liby
Club
Playing Field
OLD FARM
BANKS
GREEN LANE
GREEN LANE
ROAD
REDBRIDGE
MORETON
RO
Sand & Gravel Pits
Elliotts Pit (disused)
The Old Barn

Crossways

Summer Farm

HYBRIS BUSINESS PARK

6

Oaklands Park
THE RISE
WARMWELL
B3390
Warmwell Leisure Resort
Warmwell Country Touring Park
Skippet Heath
Hall
Enclosure

LAWRENCE PK
SCOTTON WY
HEATHFIELD PK

Pit (dis)
REDBRIDGE ROAD
RO
Tinkers Barrow
Moigne Combe Wood
LA

A   **B**   **C**   **D**

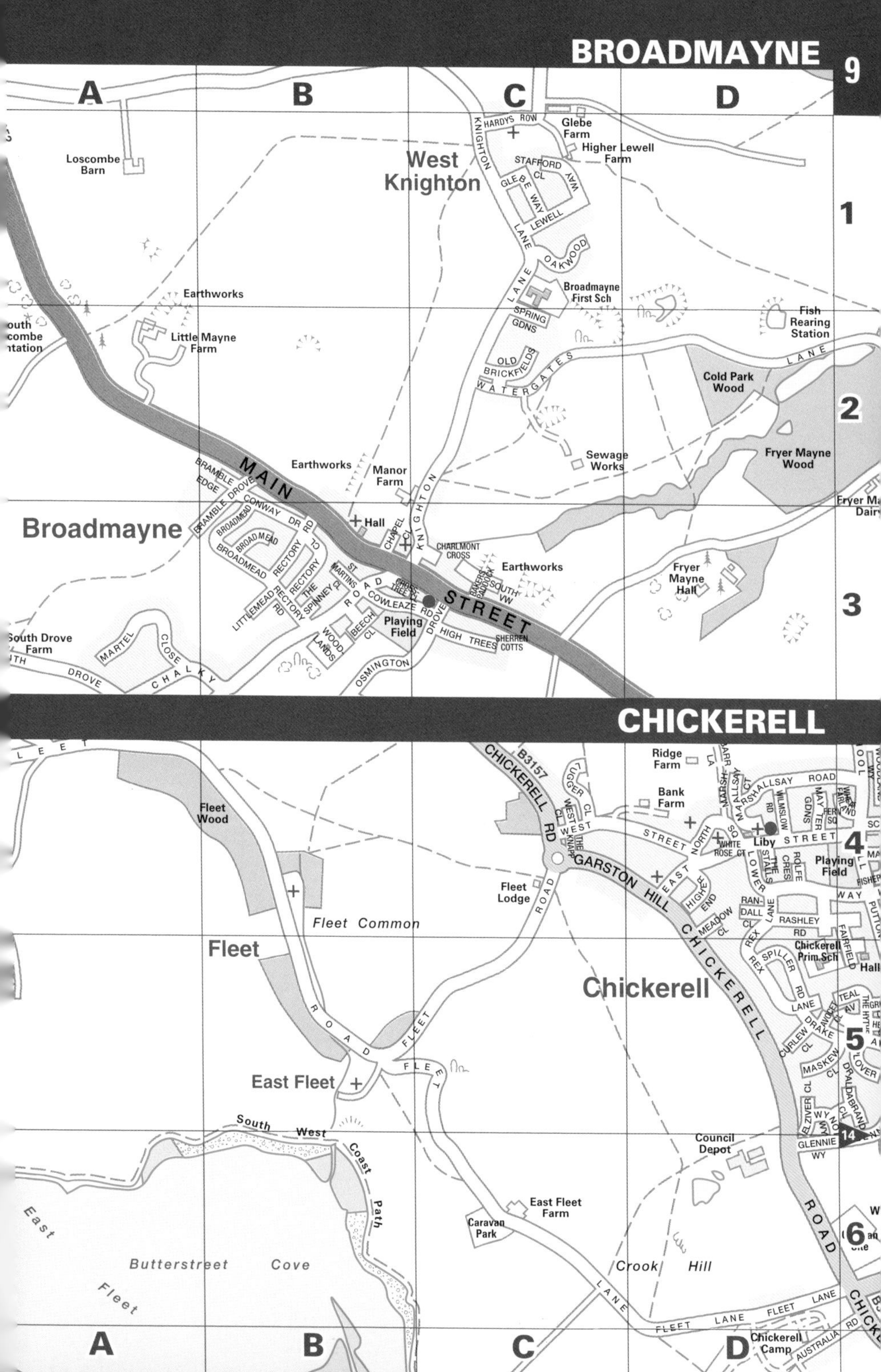

A **B** **C** **D**

Loscombe Barn

West Knighton

1

KNIGHTON

Glebe Farm

Higher Lewell Farm

STAFFORD CL

GLEBE WAY

LEWELL

HARDYS ROW

AVM

LANE

OAKWOOD

Earthworks

South combe ntation

Little Mayne Farm

Broadmayne First Sch

SPRING GDNS

OLD BRICKFIELDS

WATERGATES

Fish Rearing Station

LANE

2

Cold Park Wood

Fryer Mayne Wood

MAIN

Earthworks

Manor Farm

Broadmayne

BRAMBLE EDGE

CONWAY DR

BROADMEAD

BROADMEAD

BRAMBLE DROVE

BROADMEAD

RECTORY RD

RECTORY

LITTLEMEAD

THE SPINNEY

Hall

KNIGHTON

CHAPEL

ST MARTINS RD

CROSS TREE

COWLEAZE RD

DROVE RD

Fryer Ma Dair

Charlmont Cross

SOUTH VW

Earthworks

Fryer Mayne Hall

3

South Drove Farm

MARTEL

CLOSE

CHALKY

DROVE

WOOD LANE

BEECH

Playing Field

OSMINGTON

HIGH TREES

STREET

SHERREN COTTS

FLEET

Fleet Wood

Ridge Farm

Bank Farm

CHICKERELL RD

B3157

DOGGER CL

WEST

WEST CL

THE WHARF

NORTH

STREET

MARSHALLSAY ROAD

WHITE ROSE CT

WILMSLOW RD

EAST

MAY TER GDNS

FERN CL

SC

ROLFE CRES

STALLS

LOWER STREET

Liby

Playing Field

4

Fleet Lodge

GARSTON HILL

HIGHER

MEADOW CL

RAN-DALL CL

REX

RASHLEY RD

Chickerell Prim Sch

FAIRFIELD

Hall

Fleet

Fleet Common

ROAD

FLEET

CHICKERELL

Chickerell

REX

SPILLER RD

LANE

CURLEW DRIVE

DRAKE

TEAL

AV

5

East Fleet

FLEET

MASKEW CL

ELZIVER CL

WYN

GLENNIE WY

DRAGANRD

3

14

South West

Coast

Path

Council Depot

ROAD

6

W

Caravan Park

East Fleet Farm

Crook Hill

CHICKE

East Fleet

Butterstreet Cove

FLEET LANE

FLEET LANE

LANE

AUSTRALIA RD

Chickerell Camp

A **B** **C** **D**

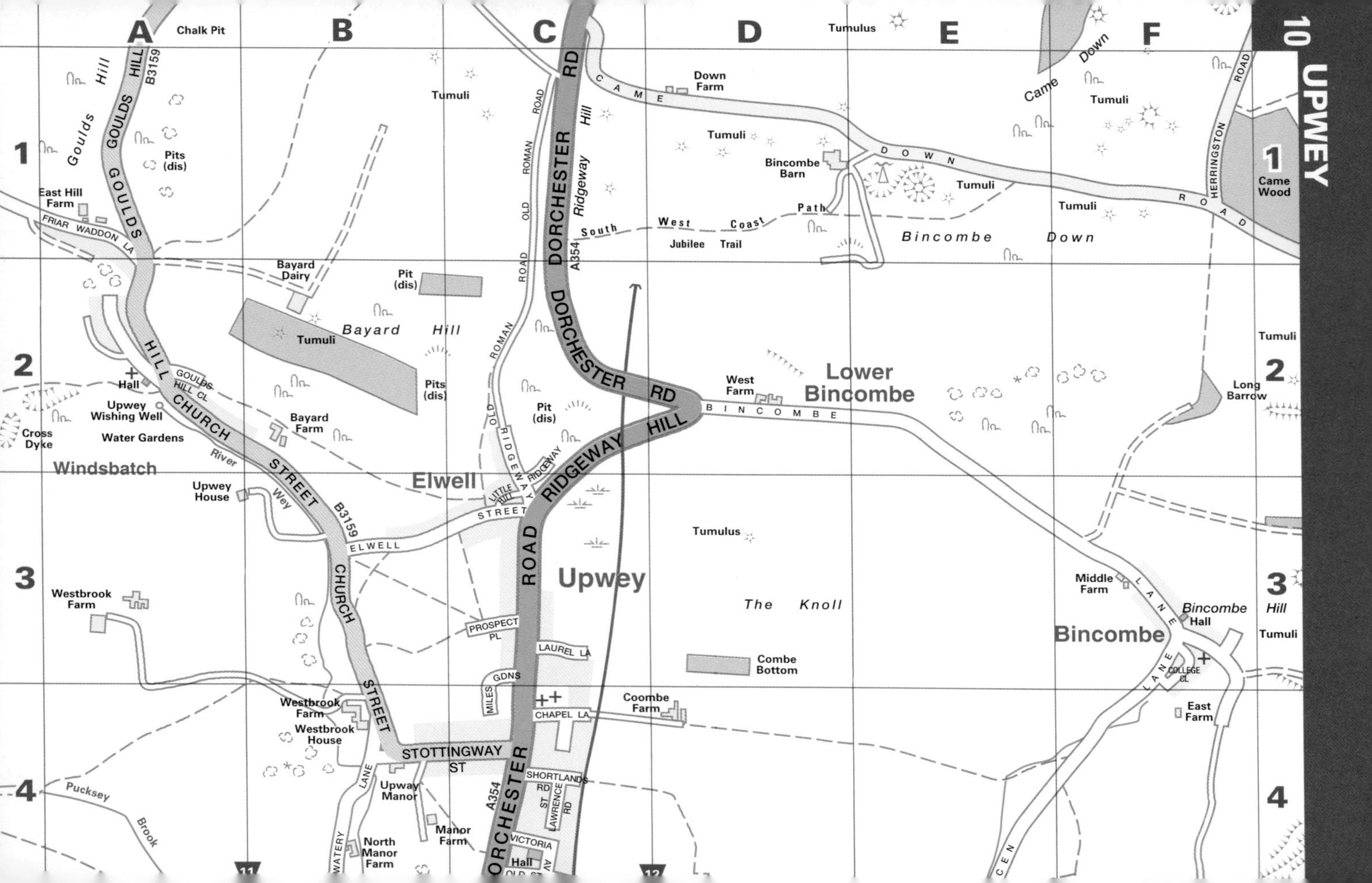

A
B
C
D
E
F
1
2
3
4
Chalk Pit
Tumulus
Goulds Hill
B3159
Goulds Hill
Pits (dis)
East Hill Farm
Friar Waddon La
Tumuli
Old Roman Road
Dorchester Rd
Ridgeway Hill
A354
Came Down
Down Farm
Came Down Road
Tumuli
Bincombe Barn
Herrington Road
Came Wood
South West Coast Path
Jubilee Trail
Bincombe Down
Bayard Dairy
Pit (dis)
Tumuli
Bayard Hill
Pits (dis)
Pit (dis)
Hall
Goulds Hill Cl
Hill Church Street
Upwey Wishing Well
Water Gardens
Cross Dyke
Bayard Farm
Windsbatch
River Wey
Upwey House
Elwell
Old Ridgeway
Ridgeway
Little Hill
Street
Ridgeway Hill
West Farm
Lower Bincombe
Bincombe
Long Barrow
Tumulus
Elwell
Road
Upwey
The Knoll
Middle Farm
Lane
Bincombe Hall
Hill
Tumuli
Bincombe
College Cl
Westbrook Farm
Church
Prospect Pl
Laurel La
Combe Bottom
Miles Gdns
Chapel La
Coombe Farm
East Farm
Westbrook Farm
Westbrook House
Stottingway St
Pucksey Brook
Lane
Upway Manor
Dorchester
A354
Shortlands Rd
St Lawrence Rd
Manor Farm
Watery
North Manor Farm
Victoria Av
Hall
Old St
11
12

Broadwey

Nottington

Redlands

Buckland Ripers

Coldharbour

A B C D

Jones Hole

Pucksey Brook

WATERY LANE

Manor Farm

THE MILL ST

Higher Manor Farm

Manor Farm

LITTLE MEAD

WEYVIEW

DORCHESTER ROAD

A354

HILLFIELD CL

CRES

BEECH

WESTLAKE RD

GEORGIAN CL

ST HELIER

ST JULIEN

MERLIN

WINSUR PL

LITTLE

1

River Wey

SPRINGFIELD RD

CRES

BRIDL

2

Holwell Farm

Brook Farm

East Farm

THE SPRINGS

LORTON LANE

THE GROVE

COURT

BROADLANDS RD

12

NOTTINGTON

Buckland House

Manor House

NOTTINGTON LANE

Nottington Farm

NOTTINGTON CT

Nottington Court

NOTTINGTON LANE

LA

A354

DORCHESTER ROAD

3

South Buckland

NOTTINGTON LANE

Egdon House

Watermeadows

River Wey

HARBOUR BRIDGE

Harbour Bridge

Corfe Hill Farm

Corfe Hill House

Radipole County Prim. Sch

Radipole Manor

WEST-MACOTT RD

STUDLAND RD

KIMMERIDGE WY

CORFE

RIDGEWAY

HOME CL

STEPLE ROAD

THENHAM

LAN-CASTER RD

We Spe

BLENHEIM

4

12

MOUNT AV

Woods View Farm

Westend Cottages

Oslers

Causeway Farm

Hall

Old Manor

RADIPOLE LANE

WEYMOUTH WAY

R C

5

Newlands Farm

North Mead Farm

COLDHARBOUR

CAUSEWAY

RADIPOLE

SPA RD

ULLSWATER CRES

AMBLESIDE

WINDERMERE CRES

LAKE SIDE GDNS

ULLS

6

Eweleaze Spinneys

GRAFTON AVENUE

RADIPOLE LANE

SYCAMO

School

SOU

CUTCLIFFE AV

SCHO

WEYMO

A B C D

14

10

A
B
C
D
1
2
3
4
5
6
10
11
15
Icen Farm
ICEN LANE
Bincombe Marsh Dairy
LITTLEMOOR ROAD
UPWEY
Broadwey
Littlemoor
Liby
Clinic & Shopping Centre
Lorton House
LORTON LANE
St. Nicholas & St. Laurence Prim. Sch
Wey Valley Sch
Coffin Coppice
Lorton Cottages
Lorton Meadows Wildlife Centre
Sports & Social Club
Playing Field
Bincombe Valley Prim. Sch
Garden Centre
Weymouth Sports Ground
Weymouth Sports Club
Weymouth Hockey Pitch
Two Mile Coppice
Horse Lynch Plantation
DORCHESTER ROAD
A354
MANOR ROUNDABOUT
Superstore
Offices
Amb Sta
MOUNT PLEASANT BUSINESS PARK
Radipole
Weymouth R.F.C
Hide
Lodmoor Nature Reserve (RSPB)
Waste Centre
Miniature Golf Course
Lodmoor Country Park
A353
WEYMOUTH WAY

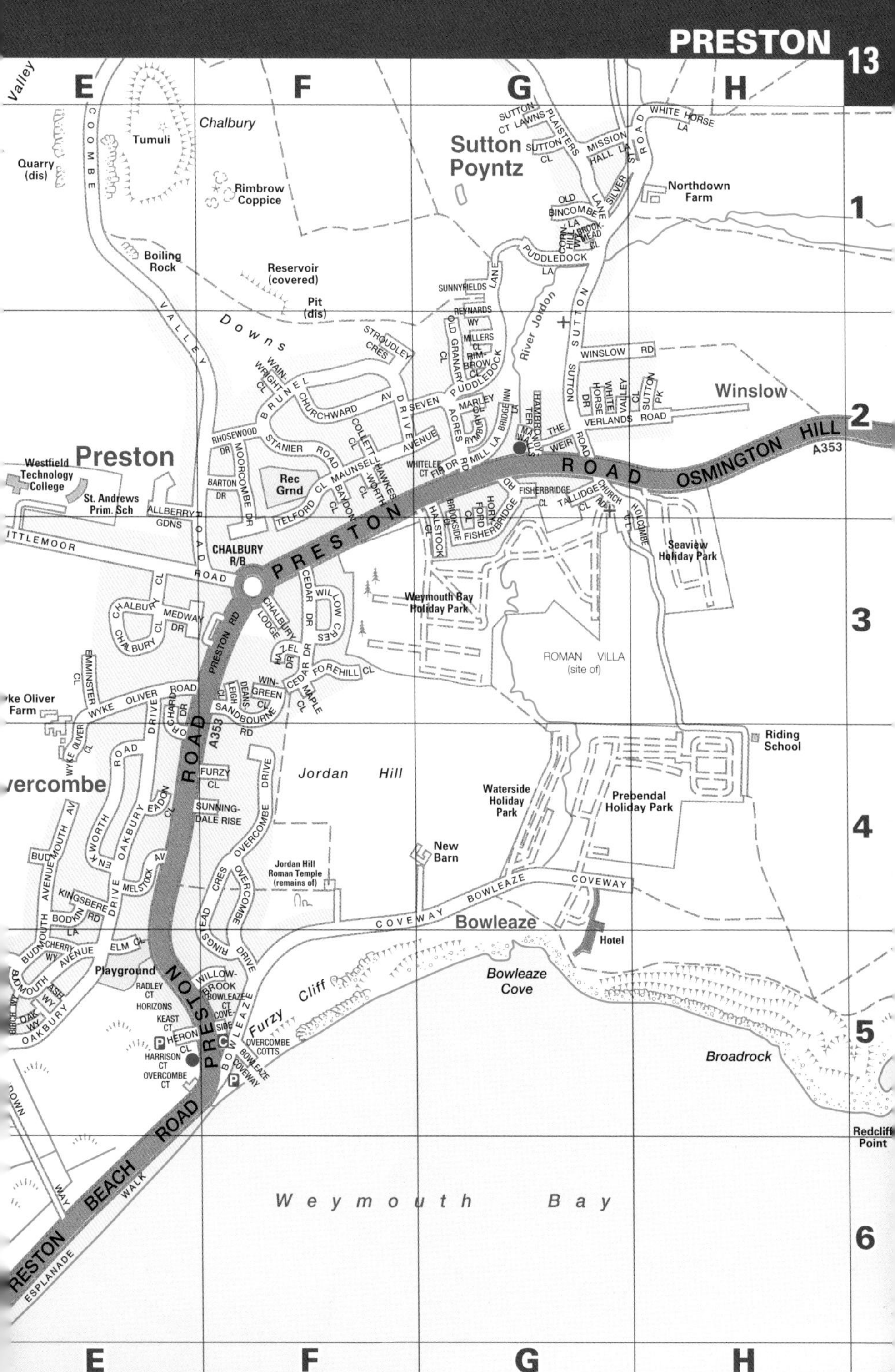

Valley

E

Tumuli

Chalbury

Sutton Poyntz

F

SUTTON CT LAWNS PLAISTERS

SUTTON CL

MISSION HALL DR

WHITE HORSE LA

G

WHITE HORSE RD

H

Quarry (dis)

Rimbrow Coppice

OLD BINCOMBE LA

BROOK-HEAD DR

Northdown Farm

1

Boiling Rock

Reservoir (covered)

Pit (dis)

SUNNYFIELDS

REYNARDS

PUDDLEDOCK LA

SILVER ST

River Jordan

SUTTON RD

WINSLOW RD

Downs

STROUDLEY CRES

OLD GRANARY CL

WY MILLERS CL RIM BROW CL

PUDDLEDOCK LA

SUTTON DR

WHITE HORSE DR

SUTTON PK

Winslow

2

VALLEY

WAIN WRIGHT CL

B R U N E L

CHURCHWARD AV

COLLETT CL

SEVEN ACRES

MARLEY CL

HAMBERLEY TER

THE WEIR

WHITEHEAD

SUTTON RD

VERLANDS

OSMINGTON HILL A353

Westfield Technology College

Preston

RHOSEWOOD DR

STANIER ROAD

HAWKES

WORTH CL

MAUNSELL

WHITELEE CT FIR

MILL LA

BRIDGE

OLD FISHERBRIDGE RD

FISHERBRIDGE CL

TALLIDGE CL

CHURCH HOLOMBE

St. Andrews Prim. Sch

ALLBERRY GDNS

BARTON DR

TELFORD CL

BANDOOR CL

ROAD

FIR

BRIDGSIDE

HALSTOCK CL

R O A D

Seaview Holiday Park

LITTLEMOOR

CHALBURY R/B

P R E S T O N

CEDAR DR

WILLOW CL

Weymouth Bay Holiday Park

3

CHALBURY CL

CHALBURY DR

MEDWAN DR

PRESTON RD

CHALBURY LODGE

HAZEL CL

CEDAR CRES

FOXHILL CL

MAPLE CL

ROMAN VILLA (site of)

ke Oliver Farm

EMMINSTER CL

WYKE OLIVER CL

RICHARD CL

WIN GREEN CV

DEANS LA

SANDBOURNE CL

Riding School

WYKE OLIVER ROAD

A353

R O A D

FURZY CL

Jordan Hill

Waterside Holiday Park

Prebendal Holiday Park

4

vercombe

WYKE OLIVER

OAKBURY DR

EATON

SUNNING-DALE RISE

OVERCOMBE DRIVE

Jordan Hill Roman Temple (remains of)

New Barn

BUD MOUTH AVENUE

EN WORTH

MELSTOCK AV

RINGSTEAD CRES

OVERCOMBE DRIVE

COVEWAY

COVEWAY

Bowleaze

Hotel

COVEWAY

KINGSBERE CL

BODN LA

CHERRY CL

ELM CL

Bowleaze Cove

5

BUDMOUTH AVENUE

ASH CL

OAKBURY

Playground

RADLEY CT HORIZONS

KEAST CT

HARRISON CT OVERCOMBE CT

WILLOW-BROOK

BOWLEAZE CV

HERON CL

COVE SIDE

FURZY

OVERCOMBE COTTS

BOWLEAZE

BOWLEAZE COVEWAY

Cliff

Broadrock

Redcliff Point

PRESTON

BEACH ROAD

WALK

P R E S T O N   B E A C H   R O A D

W e y m o u t h   B a y

6

ESPLANADE

E

F

G

H

A B C D

Southill

Putton

Charlestown

Transformer Station

Golf Driving Range

Wessex Golf Centre

East Farm Stables

Playing Field

Police H.Q.

Wessex Stadium Weymouth F.C

School

Hall

Youth Club

Chafey Lake

WESSEX R/ABOUT

GRANBY

Golf Course

The Ridgew Centr

Weymouth Golf Club

Bennetts Water Gardens

Caravan Site

GRANBY INDUSTRIAL ESTATE

LINKS ESTATE

WESTHAVEN HOSPITAL

Cerne Villa Mobile Home Park

Rawland Park

Handborough Park (Mobile Home Park)

Government Offices

Conifers Prim. Sch

Westhaven Jun. Sch

Crematorium

Cemetery

Weymouth Swimming Pool

Budmouth Technology College

Budmouth Community Sports Centre

Council Offices

Five Ways Centre

Westham

Rifle Range

Playing Fields

LITTLESEA INDUSTRIAL ESTATE

Works

Works

Wyvern Sch

Lanehouse

Furzedown Farm

Club

Littlesea Holiday Park

St. Augustines Prim. Sch

Lynch Cove

Littlesea

Superstore

JASMINE WY

A B C D

Melcombe Regis
Weymouth College
Weymouth Community Hospital
Radipole Lake Nature Reserve (RSPB)
Radipole Swannery
Bird Reserve
Radipole Lake
Jubilee Enterprise Centre
Jubilee Retail Park
Kings Roundabout
R.S.P.B Office
King St
Jubilee Clock
Weymouth Bay
Greenhill Gardens
Lodmoor Country Park
Miniature Golf Course
Miniature Railway
Sea Life Centre
Sk8 Park
Pirate Adventure Golf
Aquarium & Butterfly Farm
Sports Ground
St Johns Prim. Sch
Trimar Hospice
1. Melcombe Ct
2. Windsor Ct
3. Johnstone Ct
4. Regency Ct
Westham R/bout
Weymouth Way
Cemetery
Kings Statue
WEYMOUTH
Seacat Ferry to Guernsey, Jersey & St. Malo
Pleasure Pier
Pavilion Complex
Commercial Pier
Stone Pier
The Mixen
Nothe Fort
Nothe Gardens
Nothe Point
Barracks
CEFAS H.Q
Newtons Cove
Inner Harbour
Cineworld Cinema
Electric Palace
Shopping Centre
Marina
Liby
Lakeside Superbowl
Town Bridge
Deep Sea Adventure
Old Harbour
Tudor Ho Mus
Brewers Quay
Timewalk Museum
Harbour R/About
Superstore
Courts
Offices
Fire Sta
Weymouth Outdoor Education Centre
Running Track
Rodwell
Rodwell Trail
Rodwell Road
Westwey Road
Holy Trinit Infants Sc
Depot
Portland

A
B
C
D
1
2
3
4
5
6
14
Superstore
Garden Centre
Tented Camp
Little Bridge Farm
Pebble Bank Caravan Site
Wyke Regis
RE Bridging Hard
The Narrows
East Fleet
CHESIL BEACH
NATURE RESERVE
South West Coast Path
Hall
Cemy
All Saints C.O.E Sch
FOORDS CORNER
Health Centre
Playing field
Liby
Wyke Regis Inf. Sch
Wyke Regis Junior Sch
Recreation Ground
Community Centre
Chesil Beach Holiday Village
Jetty
Fleet Lagoon
Ferry Bridge
Chesil Beach Centre
Rifle Range (disused)
COCKLES LANE
MANDEVILLE
MANDEVILLE CL
CAMP ROAD
JASMINE WY
OVERLANDS RD
NORTH ROAD
BEACHVIEW CL
LEA RD
WYKE ROAD
LANEHOUSE ROCKS RD
B3156
PORTLAND ROAD
CRISPINS
ALL SAINTS
EBOR RD
BARROW RISE
CUNNINGHAM CL
MOUNTBATTEN CL
FOSSETT WY
BRYANTS LA
CHAMBERLAINE
WESTHILL CT
WESTHILL CL
WESTHILL RD
CASTLE HL RD
WYKE SQ
LYMES CL
WOOLAND GDNS
CHURCHILL CL
SHRUBBERY LA
COLLINS LA
KAYES CL
HAYES LANE
RODDEN CL
SWAFFIELD GDNS
LODGE
CHURCH KNAPP
BOULTON WAY
COURTAULD DR
BELFIELD PARK
BELFIELD PK DR
BUXTON ROAD
RYLANDS
HIGH STREET
WESTHILL LANE
STONEHILL CT
CHESIL VW
WEST BAY CRES
BOHAYS DR
NEW CL
FLEET VIEW RD
SOUTH ROAD
RYEMEAD LA
MARLBOROUGH AVENUE
BROUGHTON CRES
LESSINGHAM AV
WALKER CRESCENT
LANGTON AV
ELVERDAKS WY
VICTORIA RD
GALLWEY RD
PARK MEAD RD
SUNNYSIDE RD
WILLIAMS AVENUE
FAIRVIEW RD
BROADMEAD RD
BROADMEAD MW
HILLBOURNE
STOKE ROAD
DOWN CL
DONCASTER
DERWENT RD
DOVER
MERLEY RD
A354
DUMBARTON
LYNDALE RD
SANDPIPER
PLOVER
OSPREY
FERRYBRIDGE COTTS
WHITEHEAD DR
PASSAGE CL
FERRYMANS WY
SMALLMOUTH CL
PORTLAND BEACH ROAD

E F **15** G H

NEW CL
BIDWELL
MANOR
GDNS

NETHERTON
BINCLEAVES
BINCLEAVES ROAD
REDCLIFFE
VW
G epot

Holy Trinity
Infants Sch
CHURCH
ILL GDNS

A354

ROAD

KHARTOUM
ROAD

BELLE VUE ROAD
BELLE VUE
DEVENISH WARREN

Landing Stage

PORTLAND

BREAKWATER

Landing Stage

Landing Stage

Bincleaves
Groyne

1

outhlands

SUDAN RD

CLEARMOUNT

SOUTHDOWN

SOUTHLANDS

CASTLE

ROAD

UNDERBARN

WALK

Western

Ledges

Landing
Stage

ST MARTINS
ROAD
GREEN LA

WHITECROSS

LYONWELL CL

OX HENRY
CT
BOLEYN
CL
ROAD

SANDSFOOT
CT

PART WY

Landing Stage

Castle Cove

C

ST DAVIDS

ANNES
CL
ARAGON
CL
CLEVES
CL
BOLEYN
CRES
HOWARD
CL
HILLCREST
ROAD

OLD

Sandsfoot Castle
(remains of)

2

CRES

ASTER
ROAD

Weymouth
Sailing
Centre

Footwell Trail

3

P O R T L A N D

H A R B O U R

4

5

AND BEACH RD

A354

6

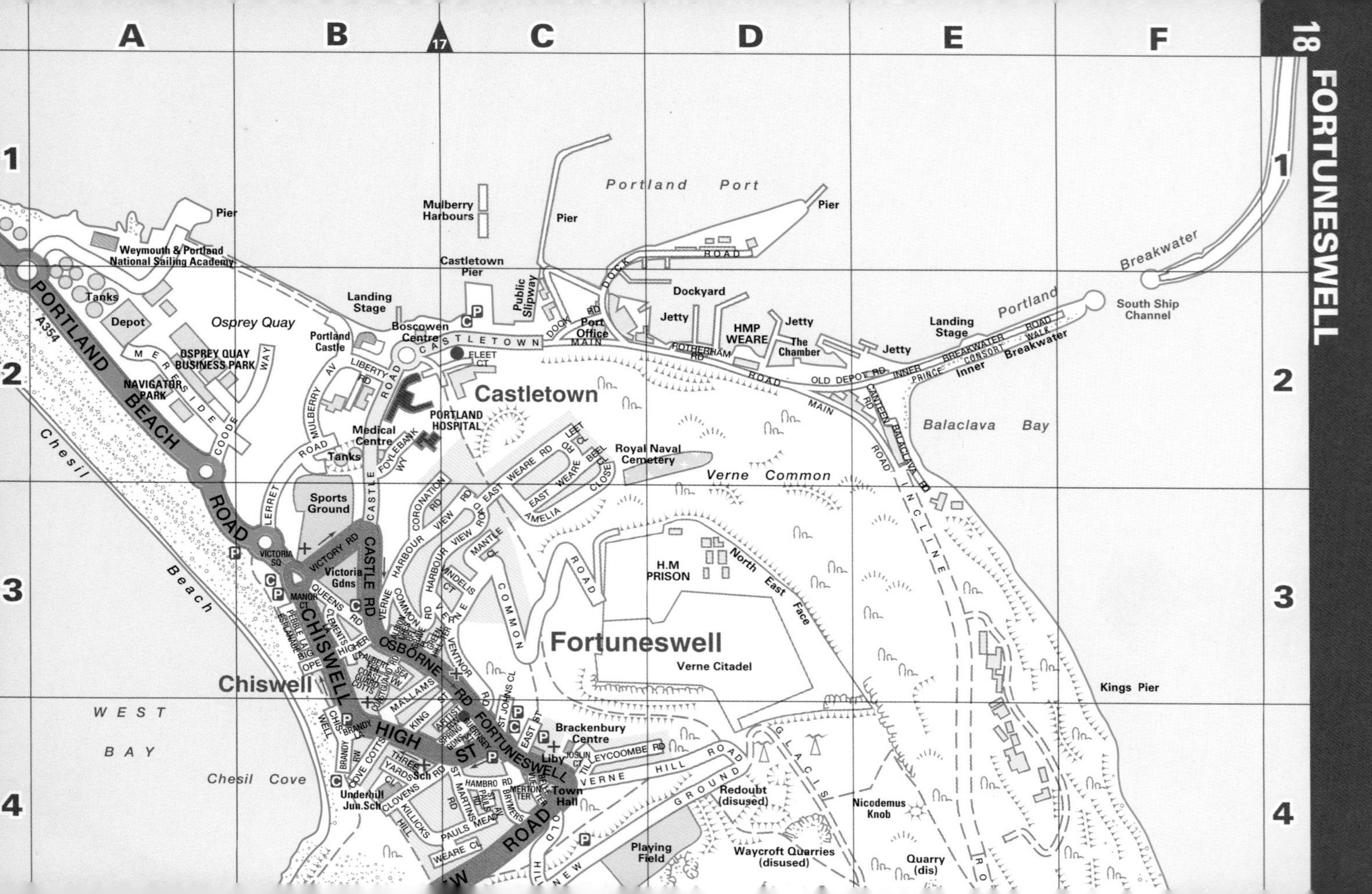

FORTUNESWELL

Castletown

Chiswell

CHISWELL

Balaclava Bay

Portland Port

Verne Common

Verne Citadel

H.M PRISON

Breakwater

South Ship Channel

Kings Pier

North East Face

Waycroft Quarries (disused)

Nicodemus Knob

Quarry (dis)

Redoubt (disused)

Playing Field

Osprey Quay

Chesil Cove

WEST BAY

Chesil Beach

PORTLAND BEACH ROAD

A354

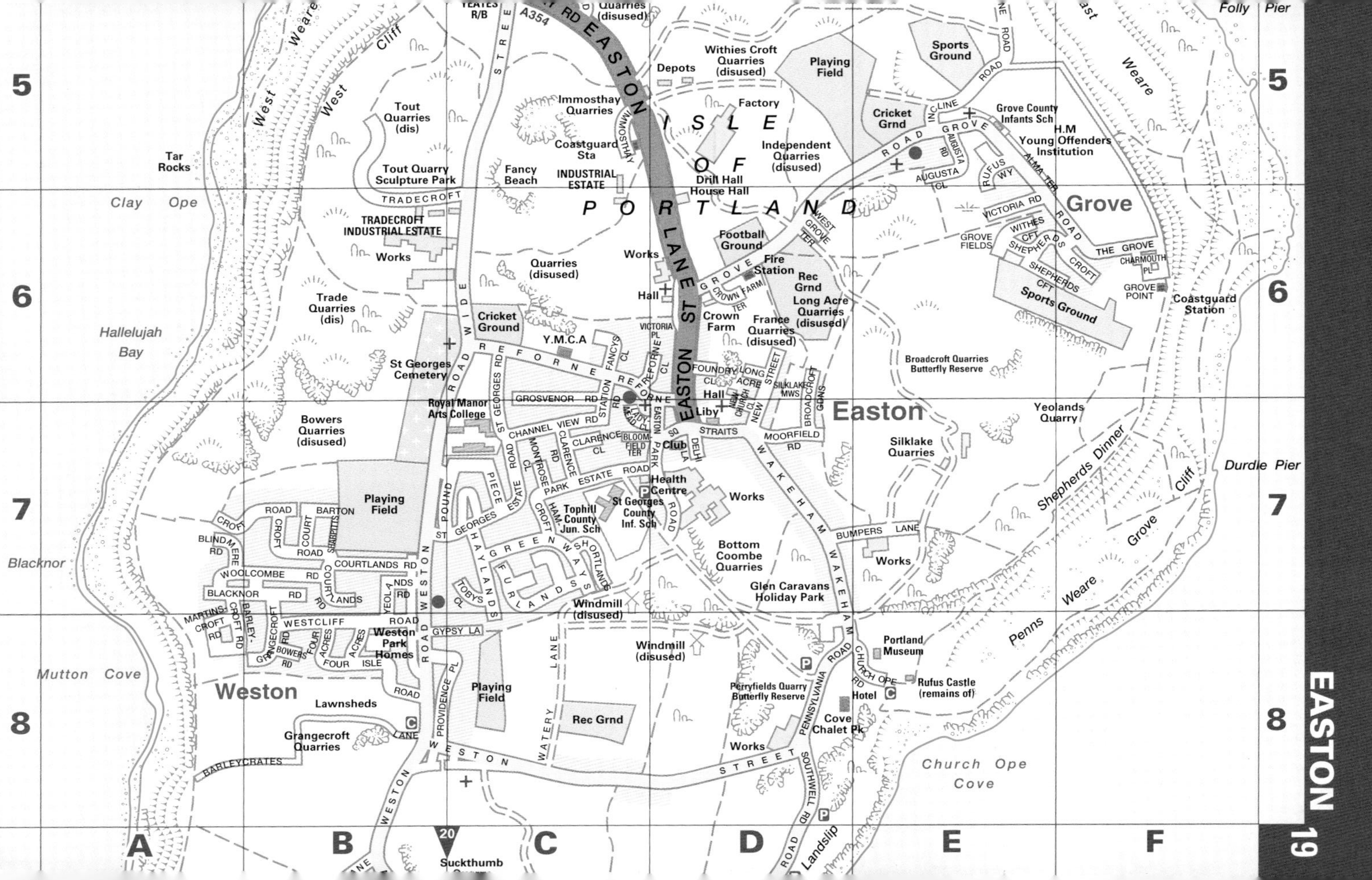

Folly Pier

Durdle Pier

Grove Cliff

Weare

Church Ope Cove

Landslip

West Weare

East

Weare

Grove

F

Coastguard Station

CHARMOUTH
GROVE POINT
THE GROVE
Shepherds Dinner

Grove
ROAD
VICTORIA RD

H.M Young Offenders Institution
Grove County Infants Sch
ALMA TER
RUFUS

WITHES
CROFT
SHEPHERDS
CFT

Sports Ground

E

Yeolands Quarry

Rufus Castle (remains of)

Portland Museum

Church Ope
Hotel
Cove Chalet Pk

Sports Ground

ROAD

GROVE
AUGUSTA
RD

Cricket Grnd

Broadcroft Quarries
Butterfly Reserve

Silklake
Quarries

Works

BUMPERS
LANE

PENNSYLVANIA
ROAD

SOUTHWELL RD

ROAD

Playing
Field

I
S
L
E

O
F

Independent
Quarries
(disused)

Rec
Grnd

WEST
GROVE
TER

Long Acre
Quarries
(disused)

BROADCROFT
RD

MWS
MOORFIELD
GDNS

WAKEHAM

Works

Glen Caravans
Holiday Park

Pierfields Quarry
Butterfly Reserve

Works

S
T
R
E
E
T

D

Withies Croft
(disused)

Factory

P
O
R
T
L
A
N
D

Fire
Station
Football
Ground

Franie
Quarries
(disused)

GROVE
TER

CHURCH
TER

CLOSE ACRE
FOUNDRY
STRAITS

NEW
STREET

LONG ACRE

WAKEHAM
ROAD

Bottom
Coombe
Quarries

Windmill
(disused)

Depots

Drift Hall
House Hall

Crown
Farm

DELHI
LA

Health
Centre

Rec Grnd

Quarries
(disused)

EASTON
ST LANE
EASTON

Hall

Works

VICTORIA
SQ

EASTON
PARK

CLARENCE
CL

PARK
ESTATE
ROAD

St Georges
County
Inf. Sch

Windmill
(disused)

W
A
T
E
R
Y

C

RD A354
R/B

Inmosthay
Quarries
Coastguard
Sta

INDUSTRIAL
ESTATE

REFORNE

FANCYS
CL

STATION

RD

GROSVENOR
RD

CHANNEL
VIEW RD
CLARENCE

Tophill
County
Jun. Sch

FURLAND
ORTLANDS

L
A
N
E

STREET

Quarries
(disused)

Y.M.C.A.

CROFT
MONTROSE

H
A
Y
L
A
N
D
S

G
R
E
E
N

WAYS

W
E
S
T
O
N

Rec Grnd

Playing
Field

WESTON

20

INMOSTHAY

Fancy
Beach

Cricket
Ground

REFORNE
ROAD

ST GEORGES
PIECE

PROVIDENCE
PL

+

Stockthumb

W
I
D
E

Tout
Quarries
(dis)

Tout Quarry
Sculpture Park

TRADECROFT

+

Royal Manor
Arts College

St Georges
Cemetery

Playing
Field

POUND

ST GEORGES
RD

ESTATE
ROAD

COURTLANDS
RD

COURT
ROAD
NDS

GYPSY LA

VEOL
YEOL

Weston
Park
Homes

Grangecroft
Quarries

B

TRADECROFT
INDUSTRIAL
ESTATE

Works

Trade
Quarries
(dis)

Bowers
Quarries
(disused)

CROFT
ROAD
BARTON
ROAD

SCARRETTS
RD

WOOLCOMBE
RD
BLIND LA

BARLEY-
MARSH'S
RD

CROFT RD

WESTCLIFF

FOUR
ACRES
RD
FOUR
ACRES
RD

ISLE
ROAD
BOWERS
RD

BARLEYCRATES
LANE

Lawnsheds

Weston

A

West Cliff

West Weare

Tar
Rocks

Clay Ope

Hallelujah
Bay

Blacknor

Mutton Cove

BLACKNOR
RD
GRANGECROFT
RD

| 5 | 6 | 7 | 8 |

A
B
C
D
1
2
3
4
5
6
19
Suckthumb Quarry (disused)
Southwell
Southwell Prim. Sch
Coombefield Quarries
Quarries (dis)
Freshwater Bay
Sweet Hill
SOUTHWELL BUSINESS PARK
God Nore
Wallsend Cove
Field System
Limekiln Cave
Sand Holes
Culver Well
Quarries (dis)
The Old Higher Lighthouse
Lloyds Cottage
Cave Hole
The Old Lower lighthouse
Rocket Post
Blow Hole
The Pulpit Inn
The Lobster Farm House
Bird Observatory
White Hole
Visitor Centre
Pulpit Rock
Land Mark
BILL OF PORTLAND
WESTON ROAD
LANE
REAP LANE
AVALANCHE ROAD
CROFT ROAD
SOUTHWELL ROAD
Southwell ROAD
HIGH STREET
ROAD
BILL
PORTLAND ROAD
PORTLAND BILL
WEST WAY
SWEET HILL
SOUTH WY
CLIFF WY
SANDHOLMES CLOSE
BARLANDS CL
SWEET HILL LANE
SEVEN ACRES
WHEATLANDS
MEAD BOWER
UNDERHEDGE GDNS
SWEET HILL MWS
LANGLEY CL
CHURCH LA
PAGE DR
CEDAR DR
WESTWOOLS
BOWN HILL
FRESHWATER CL
RUSHETTS CL
LIME KILN CL
BRANSCOMBE CL
LONGSTONE CL
CHEYNE CL
RIP
REAP LANE

Caseberry Ct DT1 4 B4
Cassiobury Rd DT4 15 F3
Casterbridge Rd DT1 5 H4
Casterbridge Trading Est DT1 5 F2
Castle Cl DT1 4 C4
Castle Hill Rd DT4 16 C2
Castle Rd DT5 18 B3
Castlemaine Rd DT3 12 C3
Castletown DT5 18 B2
Caswell Ct DT3 12 D2
Caters Pl DT1 5 E2
Catmead DT2 8 B2
Causeway DT4 11 C5
Causeway Cl DT4 11 C6
Cedar Dr, Portland DT5 20 C2
Cedar Dr, Weymouth DT3 13 F3
Cedar Rd DT1 4 C3
Celtic Cres DT1 4 C5
Chafeys Av DT4 14 C2
Chaffinch Cl DT3 12 B1
Chalbury Cl DT3 13 E3
Chalbury Lodge DT3 13 F3
Challacombe Sq DT1 4 A3
Challacombe St DT1 4 A3
Chamberlaine Rd DT4 16 C1
Chandler Cl DT3 12 B5
Channel View Rd DT5 19 C7
Channons Ct DT1 5 F3
Chapel La DT3 10 C4
Chapel Vw DT2 8 B3
Chapelhay Heights DT4 3 A5
Chapelhay St DT4 3 A5
Charles St, Weymouth DT4 15 F3
Charles St, Dorchester DT1 5 E3
Charlotte Cl DT2 7 D3
Charmile Ct DT3 12 A6
Charminster La DT2 8 A2
Charmouth Pl DT5 19 F6
Chartwell DT4 14 D1
Chaseborough Sq DT1 4 B4
Chelmsford St DT4 3 B1
Chelwood Gate DT4 14 A4
Cherry Way DT3 13 E5
Cherrybrook La DT1 4 A3
Chesil Pl DT1 5 E3
Chesil Vw DT4 16 C2
Chester Cl DT1 5 G5
Chestnut Pl DT3 12 A6
Chestnut Way DT1 4 C3
Cheyne Cl DT5 20 B1
Chickerell Rd DT3 9 C4
Chickerell Ter DT4 14 D5
Chiswell DT5 18 B4
Christchurch Ct DT1 5 E2
Church Acre DT1 5 G3
Church Cl DT1 5 F3
Church Knapp DT4 16 C1
Church La, Charminster DT2 7 C2
Church La, Portland DT5 20 C2
Church La, Stinsford DT2 6 A2
Church Ope Rd DT5 19 E8
Church Rd DT3 13 G2
Church St, Dorchester DT1 5 F3
Church St, Weymouth DT3 10 A2
Churchill Cl DT4 16 C1
Churchill Gdns DT4 17 E1
Churchward Av DT3 13 F2
Clare Av DT4 14 B5
Clarence Cl DT5 19 C7
Clarence Rd, Dorchester DT1 4 D5
Clarence Rd, Portland DT5 19 C7
Clarence Rd, Weymouth DT4 14 B6
Clarendon Av DT4 12 A4
Claudius Cl DT1 4 C6
Clayton Cl DT3 12 B2
Clearmont Ct DT4 3 A6
Clearmount Rd DT4 17 E1
Clements La DT5 18 B3
Cleveland Av DT3 12 B6
Cleves Cl DT4 17 E2
Cliff Way DT5 20 A2
Clifton Pl DT4 3 B2
Clive Ter DT4 15 E4
Clivia Cl DT3 12 C3
Clouds Hill DT2 8 B4
Clovens Rd DT5 18 B4
Clyffe Vw DT2 8 B4
Coastguard Cotts, Portland DT5 18 B3
Coastguard Cotts, Weymouth DT4 3 C5
Coastguard Rd DT5 18 B4
Cobbs Pl DT2 8 B3
Cobham Dr DT4 14 C4
Coburg Ct DT1 4 D4
Coburg Pl DT4 3 B3
Coburg Rd DT1 4 C4
Cocklands DT2 7 C3
Cockles La DT4 14 B6
Colchester Way DT4 14 C4
Coldharbour DT3 11 A6
Coleridge Pl DT4 15 F1
College Cl DT3 10 F3
College La DT4 15 G2
Collett Cl DT3 13 F2
Collins La DT4 16 C2
Colliton St DT1 5 E3
Colliton Walk DT1 5 E2
Colwell Shopping Centre DT4 3 A3
Combe Way DT2 8 B5
Comet Cl DT4 14 B6
Commercial Rd DT4 3 A2
Concorde Cl DT4 14 B6
Coneygar La DT4 3 B3
Conifer Way DT4 14 D1
Coniston Cres DT3 12 A6
Connaught Gdns DT4 15 E6
Connaught Rd DT4 15 E6
Conway Walk*, Buckingham Way DT1 5 G5
Conway Wk DT1 5 G5
Coode Wy DT5 18 A2
Coombe Av DT4 15 F1
Coombe Rd DT2 8 B3
Coombe Valley Rd DT3 13 E1
Coppice Ct DT3 12 A2
Corfe Rd DT3 11 D5
Cornhill DT1 5 E3
Cornhill Way DT3 13 G1
Cornwall Cl DT4 14 C4
Cornwall Rd DT1 5 E3
Coronation Cres DT3 12 A6
Coronation Rd, Portland DT5 18 B3
Coronation Rd, Weymouth DT3 12 A6
Corporation Rd DT4 14 D4
Corporation Yd DT4 3 A3
Corscombe Pl DT4 3 A3
Court Barton DT5 19 B7
Court Rd DT3 11 D3
Courtauld Dr DT4 16 D1
Courtlands Rd DT5 19 B7
Cove Cotts DT5 18 B4
Cove Passage DT4 3 B5
Cove Pl*, Cove Row DT4 15 G5
Cove Row DT4 3 B5
Cove St DT4 3 B5
Coveside DT3 13 F5
Coveway DT3 13 F5
Cowleaze DT2 7 B5
Cowley Cl DT1 4 C3
Cranford Av DT4 15 G1
Creech Way DT3 12 A5
Crescent St DT4 3 B2
Crispins Cl DT4 16 C1
Croft Rd DT5 19 B7
Cromwell Rd, Dorchester DT1 5 E4
Cromwell Rd, Weymouth DT4 15 E4
Cross Rd DT4 15 E6
Crossways Ct DT2 8 B5
Crown Farm Ter DT5 19 D6
Culliford Ct, Dorchester DT1 5 F4
Culliford Ct, Weymouth DT3 12 C2
Culliford Rd North DT1 5 F4
Culliford Rd South DT1 5 F4
Culliford Way DT3 12 C2
Cumberland Dr DT4 14 B3
Cunningham Cl DT4 16 C1
Cunnington Cl DT1 4 D6
Curlew Cl DT3 9 D5
Custom House Quay DT4 3 B5
Cutsome Cl DT1 5 F5

Dagmar Rd DT1 4 D4
Dahlia Cl DT3 12 C3
Dale Av DT4 15 F1
Damers Ct DT1 4 D3
Damers Rd DT1 4 C3
Dartmeet Ct DT1 4 A3
Darwin Cl DT3 12 C2
Davenport Ct DT4 15 F4
Dawlish Cres DT4 17 E2
Deansleigh Cl DT3 13 F3
Delhi La DT5 19 D7
Dennis Rd DT4 14 D5
Derby St DT4 3 B1
Derwent Rd DT4 16 D3
Devenish Cl DT4 15 F6
Devenish Gdns DT4 15 F6
Devenish Warren DT4 17 F1
Devon Rd DT4 14 D3
Diana Cl DT1 4 D5
Dick O'Th' Banks DT2 8 B4
Dick O'Th' Banks Cl DT2 8 B5
Dick OTh' Banks Rd DT2 8 B5
Digby Ct DT1 4 D4
Diggory Cres DT1 5 F5
Dinham Walk DT1 4 B3
Dock Rd DT5 18 C2
Doncaster Rd DT4 16 D3
Dorchester By-Pass DT1 4 A4
Dorchester Rd, Dorchester DT2 8 A2
Dorchester Rd, Upwey DT3 10 C4
Dorchester Rd, Weymouth DT4 15 F1
Dorset Cl DT4 14
Dorset County Hospital DT1 4
Dorset Ter DT4 3
Douglas Rd DT4 16
Doulton Cl DT4 15
Dover Rd DT4 16
Dowman Pl DT4 16
Down Cl DT4 16
Down End DT2 7
Down Rd DT4 15
Downside La DT1 4
Drake Av DT3 14
Druce La DT2 8
Druids Walk DT1 4
Duchy Cl DT1 5
Dukes Av DT1 5
Dukes Cl DT2 7
Dumbarton Rd DT4 16
Dundee Rd DT4 16
Dunnabridge Sq DT1 4
Dunnabridge St DT1 4
D'urberville Cl DT1 5
Durngate St DT1 5
Durnover Ct DT1 5

Eadon Cl DT3 13
Earl Cl DT1 5
East Hill DT2 7
East St, Chickerell DT3 9
East St, Portland DT5 18
East St, Weymouth DT4 3
East Weare Rd DT5 18
East Wyld Rd DT4 14
Eastdown Av DT3 12
Eastdown Gdns DT3 12
Easton La DT5 19
Easton Sq DT5 19
Easton St DT5 19
Ebor Rd DT4 16
Eddison Av DT1 5
Edmonds Pl DT4 14
Edward Ct DT3 14
Edward Rd DT1 4
Edward St DT4 3
Edwardsville DT4 3
Egdon Glen DT2 8
Egdon Rd DT1 5
Eldridge Cl DT1 5
Elizabeth Cl DT3 14
Elizabeth Pl DT1 4
Ellerslie Cl DT2 7
Elm Cl DT3 13
Elvastone St DT1 4
Elveroaks Way DT4 16
Elwell Manor Gdns DT4 15
Elwell St DT3 10
Elziver Cl DT3 9
Emerson Rd DT4 14
Emmadale Cl DT4 14
Emmadale Rd DT4 14

nminster Cl T3 13 E3
npool Cl DT2 8 B6
kworth Rd T3 13 E4
planade, ortland DT5 18 B3
planade, Veymouth DT4 3 C4
planade Walk T3 13 E6
sex Rd DT4 15 E4
erdene Dr T4 14 B5
erdene Rd DT1 5 F5
erest Rd DT4 15 E6
ershot Walk T1 4 C4
hibition Ct T1 5 F3

irclose DT4 15 E6
ircross Av T4 15 E6
irfield DT3 14 A2
irfield Rd DT1 5 E4
irview Rd T4 16 D2
irway Ct DT4 14 C3
iry Ct DT1 5 E2
ncys Cl DT5 19 C6
rfrae Cres DT1 5 F4
rm Cl DT4 14 D2
rm La DT1 4 B3
rringdon Cl T1 5 E5
versham DT4 14 D1
nway Cl DT1 5 H4
rn Sq DT3 9 D4
rndale Rd T4 15 F1
rnhill Av DT4 15 F1
rnhill Ter DT4 15 G1
rrybridge Cotts T4 16 D4
rrymans Way T4 16 D4
eld Barn Dr T4 14 C2
eldfare Cl DT3 12 B2
Dr DT3 13 G2
Tree Cl DT1 4 C3
recrest Cl DT3 12 A1
sherbridge Cl T3 13 G2
sherbridge Rd T3 13 G3
shermans Cl T3 14 A1
eet Ct, ortland DT5 18 C2
eet Ct, Veymouth T3 14 A4
eet La DT3 9 B5
eet Rd DT3 9 A4
eet View Rd T4 16 C2
intcomb Sq T1 4 B4
orence Rd DT1 4 D5
ordington DT1 5 F3
ordington Gdns T1 5 G4
ordington Grn T1 5 F3
orehill Cl DT3 13 F3
orest Vw DT2 8 B5
ortress Grn DT1 4 D6
Fortuneswell DT5 18 C4
Forum Grn DT1 4 C5
Fosse Grn DT1 4 C6
Fossett Way DT4 16 C1
Foundry Cl DT5 19 D6
Foundry Ct DT1 5 F3
Foundry Ct*, High St DT1 5 F3
Foundry Pl DT1 5 F3
Four Acres DT5 19 B8
Fourgates Rd DT1 4 C3
Foxglove Way DT3 12 D3
Foylebank Wy DT5 18 B2
Franchise St DT4 3 A5
Francis Rd DT4 14 D5
Franklin Cl DT4 15 E4
Franklin Rd DT4 15 E4
Fraser Av DT4 14 B6
Freemantle Rd DT4 14 B6
Freesia Cl DT3 12 C3
Freshwater Cl DT5 20 B1
Friar Waddon La DT3 10 A1
Friars Cl DT1 5 G4
Friary Hill DT1 5 E2
Friary La DT1 5 F2
Frome Ter DT1 5 E2
Frome Valley Rd DT2 8 A4
Furlands DT5 19 C7
Furzy Cl DT3 13 F4

Gabriel Grn DT1 5 F5
Gallwey Rd DT4 16 C2
Garfield Av DT1 4 C5
Garibaldi Row DT4 15 E5
Garland Cres DT1 5 F5
Garne Ct DT4 3 B2
Garston Hill DT3 9 C4
Gascoyne La DT2 7 A3
Gatcombe Cl DT1 5 G5
Geelong Cl DT3 12 C3
Gemma Ct DT4 15 E4
Georgian Cl DT3 12 A1
Glacis DT5 18 D4
Gladiator Grn DT1 4 C6
Gladstone Cl DT3 12 C3
Glebe Cl DT4 15 E6
Glebeland Cl DT2 6 C5
Glen Av DT4 15 E6
Glendinning Av DT4 15 F2
Glenmore Rd DT4 15 E3
Glennie Way DT3 14 A3
Gloucester Cl DT4 14 A4
Gloucester Mews DT4 3 B2
Gloucester Rd DT1 4 D3
Gloucester Row DT4 3 B2
Gloucester St DT4 3 B2
Glyde Ct DT1 5 E2
Glyde Path Rd DT1 5 E2
Goldcrest Cl DT3 12 B1
Goldcroft Av DT4 15 E3
Goldcroft Ct DT4 15 E3
Goldcroft Rd DT4 15 E2
Gordon Cres DT4 14 B5
Gordon Row DT4 3 B5
Goss Pl DT4 15 E3
Goulds Hill DT3 10 A1
Goulds Hill Cl DT3 10 A2
Governors La DT4 3 B4
Grafton Av DT4 11 C6
Granby Cl DT4 14 C4
Granby Ct DT4 14 B3
Granby Ind Est DT4 14 B4
Granby Way DT4 14 C3
Grange Rd DT4 15 G2
Grangecroft Rd DT5 19 B8
Granville Rd DT4 15 F5
Grasmere Cl DT3 12 A6
Grasmere Rd DT3 15 E1
Grays DT4 14 D1
Great Cranford DT1 4 A3
Great George St DT4 3 B3
Great Western Ct DT1 5 E4
Great Western Rd DT1 5 E4
Great Western Ter DT4 15 F1
Great Western Trading Est DT1 5 E4
Grebe Cl DT3 14 A2
Green La, Charlestown DT3 14 A2
Green La, Dorchester DT2 8 B5
Green La, Southlands DT4 17 E1
Greenacre DT2 7 C2
Greenacres DT2 8 A2
Greenhill DT4 15 H1
Greenhill Ct*, Melcombe Av DT4 15 G2
Greenhill Ter DT5 18 B3
Greenings Ct DT1 5 F3
Greenway Cl DT3 12 A5
Greenway Rd DT3 12 A5
Greenways DT5 19 C7
Grey School Pass DT1 5 E3
Greystones Cl DT2 8 B5
Grosvenor Cres DT1 5 E5
Grosvenor Rd, Dorchester DT1 5 E5
Grosvenor Rd, Portland DT5 19 C7
Grosvenor Rd, Weymouth DT4 15 F1
Grove Av DT4 15 F1
Grove Ct DT1 5 E2
Grove Flds DT5 19 E6
Grove Point DT5 19 F6
Grove Rd DT5 19 D6
Grove Ter DT4 15 E4
Grove Trading Est DT1 4 D2
Guernsey St DT5 18 C4
Gypsy La, Portland DT5 19 B8
Gypsy La, Weymouth DT4 15 E5

Halstock Cl DT3 13 G2
Hambro Rd DT5 18 C4
Hambro Ter DT3 13 G2
Hamcroft DT5 19 C7
Hamilton Cl DT3 12 C3
Hammond Av DT4 14 C1
Hampshire Rd DT4 14 B3
Hanover Rd DT4 15 F2
Harbour Hill DT3 11 B5
Harbour View Rd DT5 18 B3
Hardwick St DT4 3 B1
Hardy Av, Dorchester DT1 5 G3
Hardy Av, Weymouth DT4 14 D5
Hardy Cl DT2 7 B5
Hardye Arc DT1 5 E3
Hardys Ct DT4 15 F1
Harewood Rd DT1 4 A3
Harrison Ct DT3 13 E5
Hartlebury Ter DT4 3 B5
Hawkesworth Cl DT3 13 F2
Hawthorn Cl, Dorchester DT1 4 D3
Hawthorn Cl, Weymouth DT4 14 D1
Hawthorn Rd DT1 4 D3
Haydon Hill Cl DT2 7 B1
Haylands DT5 19 C7
Haylands Cl DT1 4 B3
Hayley Ct DT4 14 D5
Haymoor Cl DT3 12 D5
Haywards Av DT3 12 B6
Hazel Dr DT3 13 F3
Hazeldown Av DT3 12 D5
Headland Cl DT5 20 B1
Headland Warren DT1 4 A3
Heathcote Cl DT1 5 F3
Heathfield Pk DT2 8 B6
Heathlands Cl DT2 8 B5
Heathwood Rd DT4 15 E3
Helen La DT4 3 B4
Henry Cl DT4 17 E2
Herbert Pl DT4 3 B5
Hereford Cres DT4 14 C4
Hereford Rd DT4 14 C4
Heron Cl, Overcombe DT3 13 E5
Heron Cl, Putton DT3 14 A2
Heron Ct DT4 15 F3
Herringston Rd, Dorchester DT1 5 E6
Herringston Rd, Weymouth DT3 10 F1
Hessary St DT1 4 A3
Hetherly Rd DT3 12 B6
High East St DT1 5 E3
High St, Dorchester DT1 5 F3
High St, Fortuneswell DT5 18 B4
High St, Puddletown DT2 8 A2
High St, Southwell DT5 20 C2
High St, Weymouth DT4 16 C1
High West St, Dorchester DT1 5 E3
High West St, Weymouth DT4 3 A5
Highdown DT3 12 D5
Highdown Av DT1 4 B3
Higher Charminster DT2 7 C1
Higher End DT3 9 D4
Higher La DT5 18 B3
Highfield Cl DT2 7 B1
Highgrove Cl DT1 5 G5
Highland Rd DT4 15 E4
Hill La DT4 3 C5
Hill Vw DT2 7 B2
Hillbourne Cl DT4 16 D2
Hillbourne Rd DT4 16 D3
Hillcrest Rd DT4 17 E2
Hillfield Cl DT3 12 A1
Hillfort Cl DT1 4 D5
Hillside Ter DT1 5 G3
Hintock St DT1 4 B4
Hobart Cotts DT4 3 B5
Holbaek Cl DT1 5 G5
Holcombe Cl DT3 13 H2
Holemead Walk DT1 4 B4
Holland Cl DT4 15 F4
Holland Rd DT4 15 E4
Hollow Hill DT2 6 A1
Holloway Rd DT1 5 F3
Holly Cl DT1 4 C2
Holly Ct DT4 15 F1
Holly Rd DT4 15 E4
Holme Cl DT3 11 D5

Rundlestone Ct
DT1   4 A3
Rushetts Cl DT5 20 B1
Russell Av DT4 14 D6
Russell Ct DT1   4 D4
Rutland Rd DT4 14 D3
Ryemead La
DT4   16 C3
Rylands La DT4 16 D1
Rymbury DT3 13 G2

St Alban St DT4   3 B4
St Andrews Av
DT3   12 B6
St Andrews Cl
DT1   5 G5
St Annes Rd
DT4   17 E2
St Davids Cl
DT1   5 G5
St Davids Rd
DT4   17 E2
St Edmund St
DT4   3 B4
St Georges Av
DT4   15 G1
St Georges Cl
DT1   5 H4
St Georges Estate Rd
DT5   19 B7
St Georges Rd,
Dorchester DT1 5 G3
St Georges Rd,
Portland DT5 19 C7
St Helens Rd
DT1   4 D3
St Helier Av
DT3   12 A1
St Hellens Rd
DT4   14 B5
St James Pl DT1 4 D4
St Johns Cl DT5 18 C4
St Julien Cres
DT3   11 D1
St Lawrence Rd
DT3   10 C4
St Leonards Rd
DT4   3 A6
St Martins Rd,
Portland DT5 18 C4
St Martins Rd,
Weymouth
DT4   17 E1
St Martinsfield
DT2   7 A5
St Mary St DT4 3 B4
St Michaels Ct
DT4   15 E6
St Nicholas St
DT4   3 B4
St Patricks Av
DT4   14 B6
St Pauls Ct DT4 15 E4
St Pauls Rd DT5 18 C4
St Thomas Rd
DT1   4 D3
St Thomas St
DT4   3 B5
Salisbury Mws
DT1   5 F3
Salisbury Rd
DT4   15 E4
Salisbury St DT1 5 F3
Salisbury Ter DT1 5 F3
Salisbury Ter*,
Salisbury St DT1 5 F3
Salisbury Walk
DT1   5 F3

Samphire Cl DT4 15 G1
Sandbourne Rd
DT3   13 F3
Sanderling Cl
DT3   12 A1
Sandholmes Cl
DT5   20 B2
Sandpiper Way
DT4   16 D4
Sandringham Ct
DT1   5 G4
Sandsfoot Ct
DT4   17 E2
Sawmills La
DT1   5 E5
School Cl,
Weymouth
DT3   14 A1
School Cl,
Dorchester DT1 5 E2
School Dr DT2 8 B4
School Hill DT3 14 A1
School La DT1 5 E2
School St DT4 3 B4
Sea Vw DT5 18 B3
Seamoor Cl
DT3   12 D5
Sedgefield Cl
DT4   15 E4
Selwyn Cl DT3 12 B2
Seven Acres
DT5   20 B2
Seven Acres Rd
DT3   13 G2
Shallow Ct DT4 15 E4
Sharpitts DT5 19 B7
Shaston Cres
DT1   5 F6
Shears Rd DT4 12 B6
Sheepdown Rd
DT1   4 B3
Shepherds Cft
DT5   19 E6
Sherberton St
DT1   4 A3
Sherrings Green Cl
DT2   8 B2
Shirecroft Rd
DT4   14 D4
Shirehorse Mews
DT4   3 B6
Shirley Ct DT1 4 D4
Short Rd DT4 14 D4
Shortlands DT5 19 C7
Shortlands Rd
DT3   10 C4
Shrubbery La
DT4   16 C1
Silklake Mws
DT5   19 D6
Silver St DT3 13 G1
Slyers La DT2 5 G2
Smallmouth Cl
DT4   16 D4
Smoky Hole La
DT5   5 G4
Sodern La DT2 7 A2
Somerleigh Ct
DT1   5 E3
Somerleigh Gate
DT1   5 E3
Somerleigh Rd
DT1   5 E3
Somerset Rd
DT4   14 D3
Sorrel Cl DT4 15 G1
Souter Way DT3 12 B5

South Court Av
DT1   5 E5
South Par DT4 3 C4
South Park DT4 14 B3
South Rd DT4 16 C3
South St DT1 5 E3
South Walks DT1 5 E3
South Walks Rd
DT1   5 E4
South Way DT5 20 A2
Southcroft Rd
DT4   14 B6
Southdown Av
DT3   12 D5
Southdown Rd
DT4   17 E1
Southfield Av
DT4   15 F1
Southill Garden Dr
DT4   14 C2
Southlands Rd
DT4   17 E1
Southview Rd
DT4   14 D4
Southwell DT5 20 C2
Southwell Bsns Pk
DT5   20 A2
Southwell Rd
DT5   20 C2
Spa Av DT3 12 B6
Spa Rd DT3 12 B6
Spadger La DT2 6 D5
Spiller Rd DT3 9 D5
Spitfire Cl DT2 8 B5
Spring Av DT4 3 B6
Spring Gdns,
Portland DT5 18 C4
Spring Gdns,
Weymouth DT4 3 A5
Spring La DT4 3 B5
Spring Mews
DT4   3 A6
Spring Rd DT4 3 B6
Springfield Cres
DT3   12 A2
Springfield Rd
DT3   12 A2
Springham Walk
DT1   4 C3
Springrove Ct
DT4   15 G2
Stafford Gdns
DT2   6 C5
Stainforth Cl
DT4   14 C4
Standfast Walk
DT1   5 F5
Stanier Rd DT3 13 F2
Stanley St DT4 3 B1
Stannon St DT1 4 A3
Station App DT1 5 E4
Station Rd,
Dorchester DT2 8 C5
Station Rd,
Portland DT5 19 C7
Stavordale Ct
DT3   3 A3
Stavordale Rd
DT4   3 A3
Steeple Cl DT3 11 D5
Stinsford Business
Centre
DT2   6 A2
Stinsford Hill
DT2   5 G2
Stinsford Vw
DT1   5 G4
Stirling Rd DT3 12 A5

Stoborough Cl
DT3   12 A5
Stoke Rd DT4 16 D3
Stokehouse St
DT1   4 B4
Stonechat Cl
DT3   12 A1
Stonehill Ct
DT4   16 C2
Stottingway St
DT3   10 B4
Stowcastle St
DT1   4 B4
Stowey St DT1 4 B3
Straits DT5 19 D7
Stroudley Cres
DT3   13 F2
Studland Way
DT3   11 D5
Styles La DT2 8 B2
Sudan Rd DT4 17 F1
Sundew Cl DT1 5 G1
Sunningdale Rise
DT3   13 E4
Sunnyfields
DT3   13 G1
Sunnyside Rd
DT4   16 D2
Surrey Cl DT4 14 B3
Sussex Rd DT4 14 D3
Sutcliffe Av DT4 14 C1
Sutton Cl DT3 13 G1
Sutton Court Lawns
DT3   13 G1
Sutton Pk DT3 13 H2
Sutton Rd DT3 13 G2
Swaffield Gdns
DT4   16 D1
Swanbridge Ct
DT1   5 F2
Swannery Bri
DT4   3 A2
Swannery Ct
DT4   3 A2
Sweet Hill La
DT5   20 B2
Sweet Hill Mws
DT5   20 B2
Sweet Hill Rd
DT5   20 B2
Sycamore Rd
DT4   14 D1
Sydenham Way
DT1   5 F4
Sydney St DT4 14 D4
Symonds Cl
DT3   12 B6
Symonds Ct DT2 8 B2
Syward Cl DT1 5 H4
Syward Rd DT1 5 H4

Talbothays Rd
DT1   5 G5
Tallidge Cl DT3 13 G2
Taviton Ct DT1 4 A3
Teal Av DT3 14 A2
Tecan Way DT4 14 B4
Teeling Rd DT3 12 B6
Telford Cl DT3 13 F3
Temple Cl DT1 4 D5
Tennyson Rd
DT4   15 E5
Terminus St DT4 3 B2
The Barn DT1 5 G3
The Bindells
DT3   14 A2
The Bow DT1 5 E3

The Carriages
DT4   3
The Cherries
DT3   12 A
The Coombe
DT2   8 A
The Coppice DT3
A1
The Courtyard
DT2   8 B
The Doves DT3 12 B
The Esplanade
DT4   3
The Finches
DT3   12 A
The Green DT2 8 B
The Grove,
Dorchester DT1 5 B
The Grove,
Portland DT5 19
The Grove,
Weymouth
DT3   11 D
The Hedgerows
DT2   8 B
The Hythe DT3 14 A
The Junction
DT1   5 B
The Knapp DT3 9 C
The Maltings
DT4   3 B
The Nothe DT4 3 C
The Oak Gdns
DT2   8 B
The Orchard
DT3   11 D
The Paddock
DT2   6 D
The Rise,
Weymouth
DT4   14 C
The Rise,
Dorchester DT2 8 A
The Sawmills
DT2   8 B
The Scotton Way
DT2   8 B
The Spinney
DT3   11 D
The Square,
Charminster
DT2   7 C
The Square,
Puddletown
DT2   8 B
The Stables DT2 8 B
The Stalls DT3 9 D
The Weir DT3 13 C
The Winterbourne
Hospital
DT1   5 B
The Woodpeckers
DT3   12 B
Thompson Cl
DT2   8 A
Thornhill Cl DT1 4 D
Thornhill Cres
DT4   15 B
Thornlow Cl
DT4   16 D
Three Lanes Way
DT2   8 A
Three Yards Cl
DT5   18 B
Tilleycoombe Rd
DT4   15 B
Tincleton Rd DT2 6 C
Tinten La DT1 4 B